Peter Bell B. Ed. (Hons)

PRACTICAL TOPICS FOR THE PRIMARY SCHOOL

PART 2 HISTORY AND GEOGRAPHY

Published by:

"TOPICAL RESOURCES"

Practical Topics for the Primary School - Part 1

SCIENCE & TECHNOLOGY by Peter Bell
ISBN 1 872977 00 6
is available from all good Educational Bookshops
and by mail order from :

Topical Resources
P.O. Box 329
Fulwood
PRESTON
PR2 4SF

Copyright © 1991 Peter Bell

Printed in Great Britain for "Topical Resources", publishers of Educational Materials, P.O. Box 329, Fulwood, Preston, Lancashire, (Telephone 0772 863158), by T. Snape & Company Limited, Boltons Court, Preston, Lancashire.

Typeset by Janet Nielsen, White Cross Network, White Cross, Lancaster.

First Published May 1991.

ISBN 1 872977 03 0

CONTENTS

Introduction 1

The Background 4

The Theory 8

A Whole School Approach 21

The Approach in Practice 32

History & Geography with Nursery/Reception 42

History & Geography with Years 1 & 2 50

History & Geography with Years 3 & 4 68

History & Geography with Years 5 & 6 83

Appendix 97

INTRODUCTION

"If to plan one topic well is difficult, to organise a programme of topics successfully is almost a miracle".

The purpose of this book (the previous book and the book to follow) is to provide a simple "whole primary school" framework using Themes and Topics to help deliver the National Curriculum in Science, Technology, History and Geography with suggestions for an approach to the teaching of R.E.

This framework is intended to run parallel to existing schemes for the development of Language and Mathematics and will naturally overlap with such schemes from time to time.

The approach is built upon "good primary practice" as identified by H.M.I. in the "Aspects of Primary Education" series.

A COMMON QUOTE

The main area of weakness is in topic work. In common with this type of work in the country at large, teachers leave too much to chance in their planning and are unclear about their objectives and the opportunities for learning that need to be exploited. As a result the work is often over-prescribed, undemanding and lacking rigour.

Times Educational Supplement 19/2/88 reporting the chief H.M.I. Mr Eric Bolton's report on the performance of I.L.E.A.

Thematic work is often criticised in the Educational Press for its lack of rigour. Many people believe that it is a product of the sixties, endorsed by the Plowden Report, which will fail miserably with the introduction of the National Curriculum. The approach does in fact go back much further than that. This book will trace out its ancestry, tease out its constituent parts and explore the types of themes which can be developed in a primary school.

Those people who have already purchased "Practical Topics for the Primary School Part 1 - Science and Technology" will find that the first four chapters of Part 1 are repeated in Part 2. This was felt necessary by the author so that those people (possibly History or Geography co-ordinators) who have either only purchased Part 2, or have purchased Part 2 before Part 1, could be made fully aware of the particular approach taken to Topic Work throughout this book.

A DEFINITION OF THEMATIC WORK

Some people call it "Project Work". Some people call it "Topic" or "Centre of Interest" or "Environmental Studies". All of these terms it would seem refer to much the same sort of activity.

Thematic work is an approach to teaching in a primary school which involves various often unrelated tasks being carried out under the umbrella of a common title or "Theme" such as "Ourselves", "Pets", or "Life in the Middle Ages".

Thematic work always:
  (i)   Crosses curriculum boundaries.
  (ii) Involves practical activities.
  (iii) Uses themes selected which are thought appropriate to the interests and stage of development of children involved.
  (iv) Involves first hand experiences such as visits or visitors.
  (v)   Involves some sort of investigation.
  (vi) Involves using information gathering skills.
  (vii) Includes class, group and individual work with some elements of choice.

It should also include, if possible, an element of

"FUN".

This book begins by examining the history of the thematic approach.

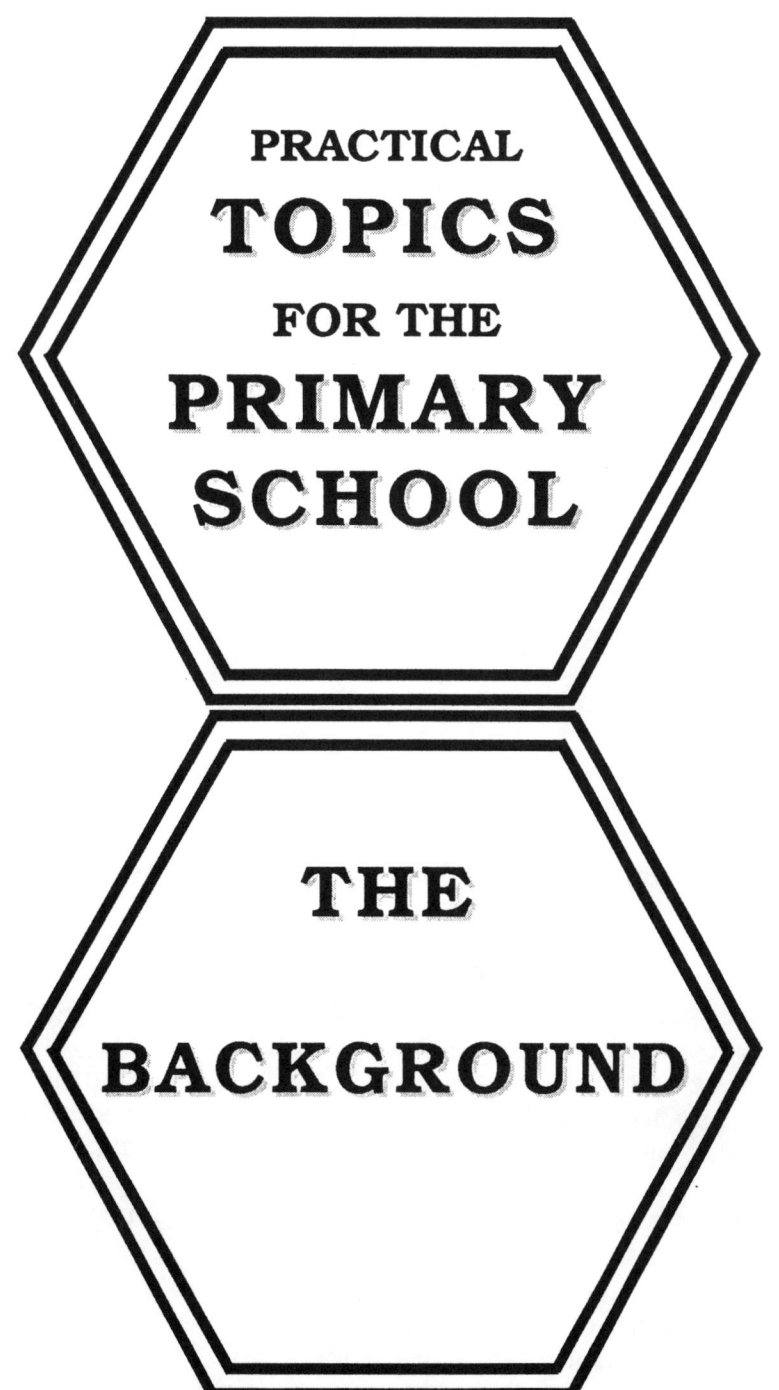

A BRIEF HISTORY OF THEMATIC WORK

The poet, Laurie Lee, describes the boredom and disenchantment of his school days as having only one aim,

to keep us out of the air and from following the normal pursuits
of the fields... Crabby's science of dates and sums and writing
seemed a typical invention of her own... prison labour like
picking oakum or sewing sacks. (1)

The so called "progressive movement" grew up in direct contrast to exposition and demonstration, generally called class teaching. Rousseau (1712 - 1728), was one of the first exponents of activity methods and favoured a highly individualised form of education. He wrote:

Teach your scholar to observe the phenomena of nature; you will soon
rouse his curiosity, but if you would have it grow, do not be in too great
a hurry to satisfy this curiosity. Put the problems before him and let
him solve them himself... let him not be taught... let him discover.(2)

Froebel (1782 - 1852) considered that the best growth occurred through varied and contrasting activities which it was the job of the educationalists to provide. His belief in activity, expressive work and the use of constructional equipment for learning was intended to penetrate all stages of education. Instead they became an essential part of of the education of nursery and infant children. Possibly "Payment by Results" was partly responsible for this as infants were literally those children below Standard 1 where children first encountered examinations.

The use of constructional equipment and sense training with the Infant age group was given further impact through the work of Maria Montessori (1870 - 1952).

At the turn of the century the ideas of John Dewey (1859 - 1952) began to influence the education of older children in the United States. He defined stages of problem-solving and suggested these as the main vehicles for learning in school. His approach led him to conclude that the whole of education could be implemented through cookery, textile making and workshop activities.

In his book "Foundation of Method" published in 1930, W.H.Kilpatrick modified Dewey's Problem Method into the Project Method.The emphasis here was on research, enquiry and discovery. He formulated four phases for the successful project: "purposing - planning - executing - judging". Again this approach was a means of involving children in purposeful activity as a learning experience.

It was to the United States that the Hadow Committee turned for information on projects. The 1931 Hadow Report on "The Primary School", which was now in theory at least, separate from the Secondary School, suggested that the curriculum should be seen in terms of "activity and experience rather than knowledge to be acquired and facts to be stored".Teachers were asked to reconsider the teaching of separate subjects in distinct lessons. However, due to a concern for the maintenance of standards, teachers were encouraged to provide an adequate amount of "drill" in reading, writing and arithmetic. Concern about mixed ability recommended that where possible, children should be streamed. Possibly this was due to preparation for the "eleven-plus" examination!

The 1933 Hadow Report on Infant and Nursery Schools was less guarded. Learning was to be individualised. Knowledge to be acquired was to derive " not so much from an instruction, as from an instructive environment". Children were to spend a large part of their school day out of doors. Learning was to be through play. Freedom was said to be essential. The child was to learn the "three Rs" only when he wanted to, "whether he be three or six years of age". (4)

In 1947 Daniel's book "Activity in the Primary School" was published and this introduced activity methods at least to the lower ends of some Junior Schools.

In 1966 the Plowden Report suggested that "Finding out has proved to be better for children than being told", (5) but it could be argued the report did not suggest a curriculum totally run along these lines.

> We endorse the trend towards individual and active learning
> and "learning by acquaintance" and should like many more
> schools to be more deeply influenced by it. Yet we certainly do not
> deny the value of "learning by description" or the need for practice of
> skills and consolidation of knowledge. (6)

The Committee also recognised the problems individualised teaching would present in a class of over thirty pupils and for economy's sake suggested that a small group of children who are roughly at the same stage might be taught together.

In 1975 William Tyndale became a by-word for all that could go wrong with modern teaching methods and it is to be noted with interest thirteen years later the T.E.S. dated 11.3.88 H.M.I. comments on the same school:

> High standards, excellent work, industry and enjoyment.
> This is William Tyndale primary school in the 1980's...
> The school is less successful in mathematics and topic work,
> which includes history, geography and religious education. (7)

The topic approach is certainly not without its problems. The use of terms such as Projects, Theme, Topic, Centre of Interest, Environmental Studies, etc. has caused much confusion over what project work is and how it can be recognised. This was clearly demonstrated when Leith (8) in 1978-9 asked thirty teachers to complete an assessment sheet which needed a clear understanding of and commitment to Kilpatrick's first principles of the approach. After two terms not one had used the procedure!

The Inspectorate paid little attention to the extent of project work in their 1978 survey report. R.E., history and geography were said to be generally taught through topics such as "helping others" or "homes". The survey itself could well be at fault here as the teacher's questionnaire on the curriculum listed only traditional separate subjects with no mention of projects. The comments it did make were not particularly encouraging:

> Taken as a whole in four out of five of all the classes which
> studied history the work was superficial. In many cases it
> involved little more than copying from reference books and often the
> themes chosen had very little historical content. (9)
>
> Similar topics, for example, "homes", or "life on the farm" or
> "children of other lands" tended to appear in classes of all ages.
> This practice can lead to unnecessary repetition unless
> considerable care is taken to ensure there is progression in
> the work which children do. (10)

In addition to the problems many teachers appear to have had in putting the approach into practice lies the government's and the Inspectorate's remarkably consistent view of the curriculum as separate subjects. This is demonstrated in their many publications on the curriculum and in much of the work by the Schools Council.

Remarkably, many teachers still appear to be committed to the project approach. Henry Pluckrose (1987) writes in his book "What is Happening in our Primary Schools" about his time as a headteacher:

> After being taken round by a six or seven year old, parents
> visiting the school for the first time were given the opportunity
> to talk to me or to one of my colleagues. The discussions rarely
> centred upon how quickly John or Sandra might master
> mathematics or reading.
> These elements of the school programme would, it was assumed,
> somehow "come". What was demanded of me, however, was
> that school would provide a secure, happy environment in which
> children would have an opportunity to share ideas, to develop
> their social skills and to discover their particular individual gifts. (11)

He defends accusations that this sounds impossible and suggests opportunities must be given for children to talk through their ideas; talk which stems from experience. He argues the primary school should:

provide a place where children can meet and talk with adults who live in and serve the local community - the fireman, the nurse, the secretary, the shopkeeper, the police officer, the craftsman and craftswoman. ...Such experiences vivify learning and give children the opportunity to talk and, through talk, to explore ideas ... Learning through first-hand experience provides the framework into which information obtained in other ways (from books, television and radio) can be fitted. (12)

The project approach is certainly able to provide opportunities for learning through first hand experience. As we move into the 1990's and the advent of the National Curriculum the whole debate about what teachers should teach and when has been taken out of their hands. This must change the emphasis from "what should I teach next" to "how am I going to teach this" and some of the many practicalities of implementing a successful whole school project approach may be solved. If the is the case, the 1990's could see the fulfilment of the educational promise of the 1960's!

REFERENCES

(1) Cider with Rosie by Laurie Lee (1962) - Crabby was his teacher.

(2) Emile by J.J. Rousseau (1762), P.131.

(3) Board of Education (1933) Infant to Nursery Schools, P.141.

(4) Ibid, P.133.

(5) Children and their Primary Schools - A report of the Central Advisory Council for Education (England) 1966, P460.

(6) Ibid, P.202.

(7) T.E.S. (11.3.88), P.6.

(8) "Project Work: an Enigma", S. Leith (1981) in Simon & Wilcocks (eds.) (1981) Research and Practice in the Primary Classroom.

(9) Primary Education in England - A survey by H.M. Inspectors of Schools (1978), P.73.

(10) Ibid, P.74.

(11) What is Happening in our Primary Schools, H. Pluckrose (1987), P.3.

(12) Ibid, P.6.

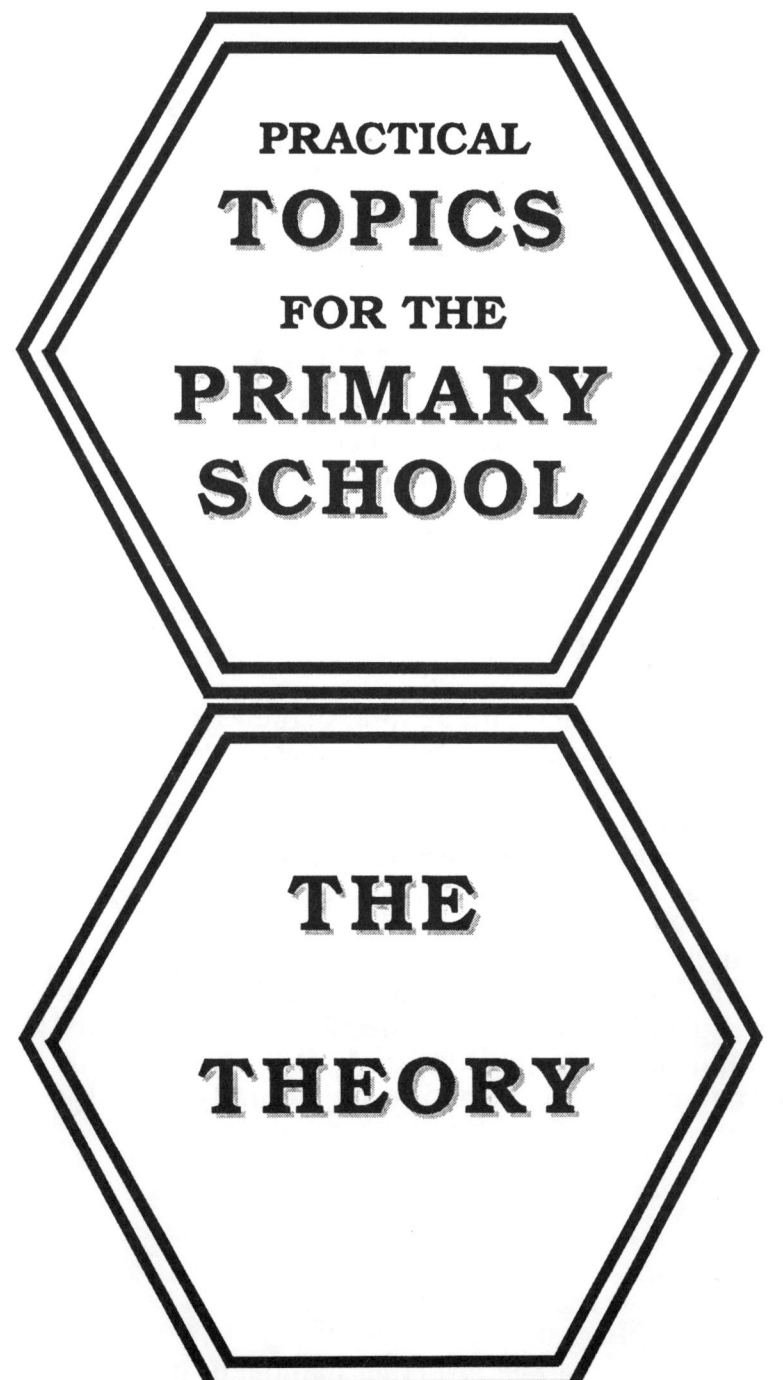

THE THEORY

You would not attempt to teach an 18 year old "A" level student in the same way as a first year pupil in a secondary school (an age difference of seven years). Similarly, you would not attempt to teach a 4 year old reception pupil in the same way as a child in Primary Year 6, (again an age difference of seven years). Consequently, the same type of Theme or Topic approach cannot be applied to all ages in a Primary School.

This section of the book will consider the factors teachers need to take into account whilst planning Themes or Topics which progress from Reception to Year 6 in the Primary School.

The first factor to be dealt with is the importance of skills and concepts.

THE IMPORTANCE OF SKILLS AND CONCEPTS

Why are skills and concepts important when planning thematic work? The Schools Council Project "Place, Time and Society" had this to say about information in today's world.

> History, geography and the social sciences are often treated as information subjects in a world in which there is an information explosion. Today's fact maybe tomorrow's fallacy. When change is the norm there is a need to provide a framework both for teachers and for children which can help them to cope with change. (13)

Skills and concepts can provide such a framework. Jerome Bruner in the early sixties argued that instruction should be focussed on developing key concepts. He saw such concepts as opening doors to the understanding of the major disciplines and facilitating further learning. Once a child had some grasp of a key concept, other newly learned material could be related to it. As well as this, Bruner and others have identified in the disciplines characteristic methods of inquiry, or skills, which could also be learned and applied to new situations. Gunning, Gunning and Wilson argue that skills and concepts must go together.

> Having acquired a concept a child needs to use it...
> "skills can hardly be practised in a vacuum".....
> "learning skills and concepts are therefore complementary activities and should go hand in hand. (14)

An examination will now be made of the nature of skills and concepts in relation to thematic work.

SKILLS

According to Science in the Secondary School Curriculum a skill is:

> the ability to perform a task, whether manual or mental, which in turn involves working out and building up a series of processes and actions into a co-ordinated sequence to be followed. A skill can be learned by repeated experience of the sequence of processes and actions making up the skill, through which understanding is gained. (15)

In a primary school there are many skills to be learned. Essential to the author's definition of thematic work is the learning of basic study or information skills which will enable the child to extract information from various written and pictorial sources. Such skills will include:

(i)	Observation	e.g. of objects, pictures, books, filmstrips, slides, maps, the environment, etc
(ii)	Referencing	e.g. using an index, contents page encyclopaedia, reference section in a library, etc.
(iii)	Oral Communication	e.g. listen, follow instructions, describe observations, recount and discuss experiences.
(iv)	Recording	e.g. present neat, well organised written work, use tables, charts, diagrams, graphs, drawings and models to supplement written work.
v)	Interpreting Information	e.g. from maps, plans, diagrams tables, charts, etc. Analyse information at a simple level and draw conclusions.
(vi)	Predicting and Hypothesising	e.g. make simple predictions, attempt to explain causes and effects and plan the next stage in own research.

In addition to the learning of study skills common to many fields of enquiry will be the learning of various modes of enquiry that are specific to individual disciplines. Henry Pluckrose writes:

> The method we adopt to arrive at an answer will be
> peculiar to the enquiry (or discipline) we are exploring. (16)

Examples of these "specific" skills are: using evidence when researching History; map-making in Geography; observation and identification in Nature Work; experimenting in practical Science; and the use of empathy in Religious Education.

David Wray (17) argues that if a project is seen as a means of teaching information skills then finding and handling particular sources of information will be a central feature of the work. Similarly, if we are teaching skills of using evidence or experimenting, then these skills too should be central features of the work. Hence using information skills and subject specific skills in an appropriate context should be part of the pupil activities to be considered when planning new thematic work.

CONCEPTS

According to Science in the Secondary School Curriculum a concept is:
> an idea under the heading of which knowledge and experience can be classified and better understood. Related items of knowledge can, therefore, be grouped together under the heading of a broad concept such as energy or a more limited concept such as heat. (18)

Together with other educationalists, Piaget and Bruner are convinced of the central importance of conceptional development in the process of intellectual growth. They suggest that success in school subjects depends substantially on conceptional development and that it is not enough to leave this to chance.

Gunning, Gunning and Wilson state that "many concrete experiences contribute to the formation of these concepts". (19), but how do we choose appropriate concrete experiences when planning our thematic work. A clue comes from Bruner's "Key" concepts. He suggests a subject is assumed to have certain characteristic or "Key" concepts which help towards the further understanding of the discipline. These "Key" concepts are what make some knowledge and experience for example come under the heading "History" and other knowledge and experience for example under the heading "Science".

Examples of "Key" Historical concepts could be:
- Past and Present.
- Continuity and Change.
- Sense of Chronology.
- Cause and Consequence.

Examples of "Key" Scientific concepts could be:
- Energy
- Materials
- Environment
- Alive and Dead

Inseparable from the idea of key concepts is that of Bruner's spiral curriculum. I quote:
> "children will first encounter key ideas and concepts in a primitive form in early childhood, and will re-encounter them in a more highly developed forms in their subsequent work in schools, each encounter leading to a more sophisticated understanding." (20)

Hence in our planning of thematic work it must be ensured "Key" concepts of the disciplines are introduced using concrete experiences at an early stage so that these concepts can be built upon using progressively more sophisticated experiences on a regular basis.

Bruner claims that his approach to teaching the concepts and skills which characterize a discipline means that "the foundations of any subject can be taught to anybody at any age in an intellectually respectable form". (21)

A teacher's goals must therefore be to develop the skills and concepts appropriate to the pupil's stage of development through a content of interest to the age group.

THE NATURE OF THE "YOUNG CHILD" AND HIS WORK

What is a young child in a Primary School? British legislation states that a child must attend school full time during the school term following his/her fifth birthday.

Practice varies throughout the county with many local education authorities admitting children before they are five years old. From September 1987 Lancashire's policy has been to admit children to primary school in the September of the academic year the child is five years old. This means that the youngest primary children are barely four years old!

What is the "nature" of such a child? A quote from a reception class teacher in "Starting School: An Evaluation of the Experience" gives a clue to some of the needs that must be catered for.

> I really don't think teachers who have never taken
> reception classes appreciate the problems. They think
> you are just there to supervise them. They don't really
> realize the problems that you have to cope with as well
> as teaching them basic things. (22)

The report goes on to identify "survival skills" children need to learn, know and use in order to function confidently in the classroom. They include often assumed skills such as knowing who they are, what they can do and how to cope with and overcome "not knowing" things and the feelings this arouses. Six other skills were also listed.

A L.E.A. Early Admissions Document considers the following may be worth remembering:

> they have been constructing and speaking in sentences
> for only a year or so.
> their hand/eye co-ordination and fine motor skills are
> still developing.
> they are physically active.
> they are at the intuitive stage of development,
> finding difficulty in eeing another's point of view
> or dealing with the abstract.
> they can be capable of periods of concentration but
> may never have had the opportunity to develop this so
> appear to flit from one activity to another, or cruise around
> in an apparently aimless way.
> they may never have had the opportunity to mix with a
> large group of children of the same age.
> they may never have experienced being left with adults
> unfamiliar to them.
> new situations and experiences can be a stimulus and
> challenge to some but a threat to others. (23)

The author's own experience has found that when they arrive at school they cannot read and write and during the time spent accomplishing these skills much effort is needed by each individual for relatively modest results in these areas, a phenomenon which is little understood by teachers of older children. A short spell trying to teach middle infants science with what I thought very simple worksheets which required detailed written answers soon showed me the error of my ways!

In addition to this, each child is an individual. Ability to accomplish tasks will vary according to stage and rate of development, home environment and breadth of experience to date. The reception class teacher's task is surely a very difficult one indeed.

So what sort of "work" should these young children be presented with when they arrive at primary school? The answer to this question will depend not only on how we perceive the "nature" of our young children but also upon our understanding of how they learn.

Tina Bruce (24) suggests there are three ways of looking at this.
- (a) The Empiricist View which suggests the child is an empty vessel to be filled.
- (b) The Nativist View which suggests children are pre-programmed to unfold in certain directions.
- (c) The Interactionist View which suggests children are partly empty vessels and partly pre-programmed and that there is an interaction between the two.

In reality the early childhood tradition has not taken the extreme stances of the Empirist or the Nativist. Recent support for the Interactionist point of view comes from Tom Bower who claims that development occurs as:

"environmental events interacting with maturationally generated behaviours. The major causal factors in cognitive development are behaviours interacting with other behaviours in their application to environmental events". (25)

This suggests that a child interacts with its environment <u>and</u> within itself. Consequently, adults are not seen as instructors purely giving our information and knowledge but more as the means by which children can develop "their own strategies, initiatives and responses, and construct their own rules which enable their development." (26) Children are supported by adults who help them to make maximum use of the environment.

An appropriate environment for four year old children in school can be envisaged by examining suggestions for equipment made in an L.E.A.'s Early Admissions Document.

They include:-

(1)	Outdoor Play Equipment	e.g. slide, climbing frame, carts. trolleys
(2)	Sand Play Equipment	e.g. wet sand, dry sand, rakes, spades, sieves, scoops, etc
(3)	Water Play Equipment	e.g. water tray, sponge, cork, boats, watering can, etc
(4)	Home Corner Equipment	e.g. sink, bed, dolls, table, mirror, telephone, etc
(5)	Imaginative Play Equipment	e.g. dressing up clothes, puppets, train set, dolls house etc.
(6)	Book/Library Corner	e.g. books, visual aids, photograph albums, magazines, etc.
(7)	Creative Area	e.g. paper, paint, pens, crayons, printing/collage materials, scissors, etc
(8)	Table Apparatus	e.g. constructional toys, jigsaws, fuzzy felts, dominoes, etc
(9)	Floortoys	e.g. large jigsaws, farm, bricks, crane, trucks, etc.
(10)	Science	e.g. magnets, magnifying glass, wormery, fish tank, bulbs, etc.
(11)	Musical Instruments	e.g. drums, triangles, home made instruments, tape recorder, etc.

Tina Bruce's examination of the work of Froebel, Montessori and Steiner enabled ten common principles of an "early childhood tradition to be drawn up". The author has selected three principles which help us decide on appropriate adult support for children in the early years. The first selection considers planning a theme.

Principle No 3
"Learning is not compartmentalised, for everything links". (27) The aim of nursery and infant school teachers is to provide children with integrated learning experiences rather than to fragment these experiences into subject-based areas. However, flexibly interpreted, subject boundaries can help the teacher to select and plan activities to promote distinctive sets of skills within an appropriate framework.

Dave Fontana states:
> all the experiences encountered by a child have a
> potential influence upon his long-term development.
> Thus these experiences cannot be viewed simply as ends in
> themselves, but should be seen within the context of this
> development, and should be chosen by the teacher with
> an eye to those forms of development which society considers
> to be most worthwhile. (28)

Hence even the teacher of the youngest children in school needs to consider simple study skills; at this stage purely language skills, very simple subject specific skills and key concepts to lay the foundations of Bruner's spiral curriculum. Examples of appropriate experiences could inclide a museum table with old and new objects, regular discussion, handling and change of items. This would be the beginning of historical enquiry. Regular play with different road map scenes or models such as farmyards or villages could promote geographical work. A number of seasonal walks over the course of a year could promote work on nature. Play with water, sand and constructional toys could form the basis of science and technology. Discussion of social issues when and where they arise could be the basis of R.E.

The second selection considers where to start.

Principle No 7
"What children can do (rather than what they cannot do) is the starting point in the child's education." (29) The job most children understand well is how to play. Plato saw play as a means of teaching children the skills of adult work. Comenius recommended education based on learning by doing: "Whatever children delight to play with... provided it be not hurtful, they ought rather to be gratified than restrained from it" (The School of Infancy, 1633). (30)

Children learn about materials by playing with them and continue to learn more at different levels in intellectual growth. A child develops notions of right and wrong behaviour with the help of social play. As a result of these different kinds of learning, the child is constantly forming ideas about the world and about the way in which it works. Through play with materials and people he develops concepts and learns to use thinking skills, the building blocks of the spiral curriculum.

Examples of such learning could include sand and water play in the homecorner.

The third selection considers the type of support the child needs.

Principle No 9

"The people (both adults and children) with whom the child interacts are of central importance." (31) Manning and Sharp suggest that provision of opportunity and materials is not sufficient to provide cognitive learning experiences. They state:
> Without the help of a teacher setting the environment and
> providing the suggestions, children reach stalemate and their
> play becomes intellectually aimless... A skilled teacher can
> point the children's enquiry, provide new materials, stimulate
> discussion or bring out new possibilities in an existing situation. (32)

The teacher promotes physical, social and emotional development through participation, initiation and intervention in a child's play. Great sensitivity is needed in deciding when to join in and what kind of contribution may be helpful.

A child involved in "Circus" or "Farm" role play for example can be encouraged to talk out what he is doing to help him establish concepts and to acquire vocablulary. This then becomes part of his thought processes; further building blocks in the spiral curriculum!

What content is appropriate to the work of the young child? As mentioned earlier they are at Piaget's intuitive stage of development.
The Science 5 - 13 series suggests that at this stage appropriate objectives are "those concerned with active exploration of the immediate environment". (33) This, and also making use of individual or group interests can help in the selection of appropriate content.

Themes centred on a child's local environment could include "Ourselves", "My Family", "Babies", "Model Town", "Old People", "My last 5 years", "Our School", "The Circus", "The Zoo", "Down the Street", "Creepy Crawlies", "Growing Things", etc.

All of these themes can provide opportunities for visits or visitors and hence development of language work, stimulus for various types of play, ideas for table apparatus and many creative activities.

In conclusion the young child's work should include:
(1) An appropriate learning environment which provides much practical experience.
(2) Cross-curricular learning experiences which have been planned with long-term development in mind.
(3) Tasks which begin with what young children can already do well - play!
(4) The intervention of an extremely sensitive adult capable of developing children's play.
(5) Exploration of themes based on the child's immediate environment and interests.

PLAY AND THE SUBJECT DISCIPLINES

What is play? The Oxford Dictionary has a large selection of terms which describe play including: "Move about in lively or unrestrained manner... activity... pretend for fun". (34) It can be an extremely emotive word especially when an anxious parent asks his/her young child about what they did at school and receives the answer "Oh we played all day", instead of correctly answering "I engaged in a series of carefully worked out practical activities which lay the foundations of key concepts in the subject disciplines!"

What are subject disciplines? Hirst and Peters (35) broke knowledge down into the following areas: Philosophy, Moral judgement and awareness, Human studies, Religious understanding, Formal logic and mathematics, Physical sciences and Aesthetic experiences. In practice, Secondary Schools use the more familiar terms: History, Geography, Religious Education, Mathematics, Science, Art, Music, Physical Education and Craft. The advent of the new G.C.S.E. examination has revolutionised much course work with the emphasis moving away from memorising facts to using characteristic modes of enquiry as suggested by Bruner. The pupils are asked to "act out" the role of the Historian, the Geographer or the Scientist instead of just being passive recipients of numerous facts. In short, they are "playing at or pretending to be the real thing."

What sort of "play" is appropriate to develop these characteristic modes of enquiry? To answer this question we must examine the subject disciplines individually.

History

Joan Blyth in her book "History 5 to 9" (36) suggests History teaching should include the following elements:

Using Evidence	e.g. Pictures, photographs, newspapers, taped interviews, books, museums, old buildings, etc.
Handling Artifacts	e.g. old fashioned household objects reproduction jewellery, costumes or armour, etc.
Use of a Time Line	e.g. placing objects or events in chronological order without worrying about specific dates.
Use of the Narrative	e.g. Rosemary Sutcliff's stories of the Roman Legions. Visiting museums and old buildings.
Using appropriate vocabulary	e.g. Stone age, Medieval, Victorian etc.
Use of Empathy	e.g. using role play to attempt to put oneself into anothers shoes.

Use of these techniques will help to develop the characteristic modes of enquiry of the Historian, skills which can then be used to explore key historical concepts such as:

>Past and present.
>Continuity and Change
>Sense of Chronology
>Cause and Consequence

Geography

The H.M.I. Curriculum Matters Booklet No 7 "Geography from 5 to 16" (37) suggests the primary curriculum should include:

Investigations of the local environment	e.g. surface features, activities of inhabitants, weather etc.
Study of life and conditions in Britain and abroad	e.g. compare small areas of Britain or abroad with own locality.
Acquaintance with a variety of maps	e.g. O.S. Maps, historical maps, large scale of own neighbourhood, etc.
Techniques of map reading and interpretation	e.g. work on scale, co-ordinates, etc.
Familiarity with globes and with atlas maps.	e.g. identifying continents oceans, countries, etc.

Of interest is a piece of research by Blades and Spencer which states: "untrained children as young as 3 years old can use maps to locate places in small environments, and that after the age of 4 - 5 years many children can use a map to follow a route". (38)

Use of maps and map skills will help to develop the characteristic modes of enquiry of the Geographer, which in turn can be used to explore key Geographical concepts such as:

>Similarity and Difference
>Spatial Relationships
>Communication
>Cause and Consequence.

Science

The H.M.I booklet "Primary Education in England" (39) described a curriculum model which split Science into two main areas, Experimental Science and Observational Science. This is a useful way of dividing up such a large area of the curriculum.

Experimental Science.
"Lancashire looks at Science in the Early Years" states that:
"Science is the study of the world about us carried out in a
particular way... the scientific method." (40)
This "scientific method" describes the way in which scientific investigations are carried out and includes:

Making observations e.g. a twisted elastic band connected to a propellor makes a model boat move.
Asking questions e.g. how far will the boat move with 25 twists?
Experimenting e.g. carrying out the task and recording the results.
Deducing and coming to conclusions about what has happened based on evidence, e.g. thinking about what actually happened and why. This can lead to the whole process being repeated possibly reaching a general conclusion.
Working in this way teaches the characteristic modes of enquiry of the Experimental Scientist which can be used to explore such key scientific concepts as Energy, Materials and Ourselves.

Observational Science
Observational Science would seem to include those areas of science which are either impossible or unethical to experiment with in the primary school such as animals or the enviromnent. Even though children are unable to experiment in these areas, my experience has shown they do have much intrinsic fascination for children and hence can be used for promoting the skills of careful observation, and identification using simple scientific keys and reference books.
Working in this way promotes the characteristic modes of enquiry of the "Naturalist" which can be used to explore such key concepts as Environment and Alive/Dead.

Religious Education

The teaching of religion in primary schools was originally called Religious Instruction and was concerned with learning the Christian faith in a similar way to contemporary Sunday School. Gradually the name changed to Religious Knowledge (or Scripture), which was content based but looked at other faiths as well as Christianity. More recently the term Religious Education has been used which promotes an awareness of the spiritual side of life within an educational framework. The Schools Council Publication "Discovering and Approach" states:
religious education should have two sides to it. It is to help children
understand the religious traditions of life and thought that they
meet in their environment. It is also to help children to be sensitive to
the ultimate questions posed by life and to the dimension of mystery
and wonder that underlies all human experience. (41)
The Westhill Project R.E. 5 - 16 by Read, Rudge and Haworth (42) is an example of such an approach. They suggest three sources of content which interact with each other:

(1) Traditional Belief Systems, e.g. exploration of religious beliefs and practices. The project suggests that there is no need to explore all six major traditions in the primary school in equal measure: Christian beliefs and practices could be taught with examples drawn from the other faiths to show comparison. Empathy is an important skill to develop here!

2) Shared Human Experiences: e.g. examination of common experiences such as birth, death, joy, sadness, fear, frustration can lead to exploration of "Ultimate Questions" such as "Do people matter more than things? or "What is love?".

(3) Individualised Patterns of Belief in the Classroom: e.g. "But I don't believe in God Miss!" How these emerge or become material for exploration is entirely informal and ad hoc. An objection may arise in discussion or a child may point out a different way of looking at something. The sensitive teacher will always be looking for opportunity to include and develop these more personal and individual contributions in a way which will benefit the whole class.

Working in this way "touches" on the characteristic modes of enquiry of the Theologian which can be used to explore such key Theological concepts as Self, Religious Traditions, Human Experiences and Choice.

Technology

Technology is a recent addition to the primary currriculum as a seperately identifiable subject. The government definition includes what was known in Secondary Schools as Craft, Design and Technology, Business Studies, Home Economics, Art, and Information Technology. Craft is a combination of Woodwork, Metalwork and work with plastics. Design involves Technical Drawing and a process in which the pupil has to:
> identify the need to be met, assemble any relavant information,
> and evaluate the effectiveness of the solution. (43)

Technology is the "application of science". (44) Once a problem has been identified and researched a solution is proposed. The pupil is then required to build a "device" or "machine" which will fill the need. Business Studies would involve the pupils in considering commercial applications for their designs. Cookery, Art Work and use of Computers are all tools or skills which could be involved in arriving at "a solution to an identified problem".

The skills involved are:
(1) Identifying a need.
(2) Devising a solution to the need taking into account the reason for the problem to be solved and the availability and cost of appropriate materials.
(3) Making notes and detailed drawings of the solution.
(4) Constructing objects/ sets of objects/ surroundigs from the design making good use of appropriate tools and materials.
(5) Improving the performance of the solution and commenting on the final outcome

Working in this way promotes the characteristic modes of enquiry of the "engineer" and/or "business man" which can be used to explore key scientific concepts such as Energy, Materials and Environment.

How can these modes of enquiry by systematically organised into a programme of work(or is it play?) for primary aged children? The answer it could be argued is to use a series of Themes or Topics which vary in nature according to the stage of development of the children involved. Piaget's stages of development would suggest that eleven year old children do not learn in the same way as four year old children.

As discussed earlier, the youngest children in primary school learn from interaction with the environment and within themselves. Appropriate Themes are totally cross-curricular but subject disciplines should be considered when planning activities which become part of their environment.

The oldest children in the primary school are about to enter the Secondary system and encounter its isolated subject disciplines.

Several years of experience using half termly Themes with a definite bias towards one specific subject discipline has in the author's opinion provided good preparation for the future. Working in this way can avoid common pitfalls of the project approach such as lack of structure; avoidance of unfamiliar areas of the curriculum and contrived work which attempts to bring all areas of the curriculum into one theme. It is also an ideal way of using a theme which will develop a specific mode of enquiry or specific skills which can be used to explore appropriate concepts.

An example of such a theme could be a Geography Project on "The Netherlands". Study skills such as using an index, school library, personal interviews, etc. could be developed based on a geographical content. As well as this, specific geographical skills such as "mapping" would be developed. Other curriculum areas <u>are always encountered</u> in each study, for instance, Drama Work, Language Work, Mathematics and Creative Activities could appear in any project, but the emphasis would be on developing skills specific to the main theme.

However, a complete programme could not be based on totally cross-curricular themes for Infant children and subject biased themes for Junior children. Again, referring to Piaget's stages of development as outlined in "With Objectives in Mind". (45) Four stages are mentioned, not two! They are:

(1) Transition form intuition to concrete operations.
(2) Concrete operations early stage.
(3) Concrete operations later stage.
(4) Transition to abstract thinking.

Mentioned earlier was a stage where young children are just beginning to read and write. Joan Blyth, when writing about teaching history to young children, states:

"study of the past can motivate children to want to read,
particularly as 7 and 8 year olds outgrow picture reading and
one-sentence explanations of their own pictures". (46)

Mollie Jenkins, a teacher and parent, eventually started her own school because of her dissatisfaction with the type of education schools offered her own children. She writes:

Now that the children could read, the real fun of learning
could begin, although we still spent a brief period each morning
on the sheer mechanics of reading and writing (phonetics and
work-building, spelling, writing-practice, and so on). For the rest
I just let them loose on the largest and most exciting collection of
books that I could muster and waited to see what would emerge.
All sorts of things did, and developed in the most exciting way". (47)

It could be strongly argued that this is the time to introduce studies where young children are attempting to make a sytematic investigation of aspects of the world around them.. Much of the work will be oral, possibly based on local visits to the fire station, the shops, etc. Play activities must be built in to help the children "internalise" new information, but the children will also be motivated to read more and eventually write about their experiences.

Themes with a "<u>slight</u> leaning" towards a subject discipline could provide the framework for such an enquiry. Examples could be The Museum (History), The Fire Station (Geography), Pets (Nature), The Church (R.E.), etc Such themes may be developed in any direction according to the childrens interests, but would still provide a simple framework to include simple subject specific skills.

The three types of theme outlined;
(i) the totally cross-curricular theme,
(ii) the theme with a "slight leaning" towards a subject discipline, and
(iii) the theme that has a definite bias towards a discipline, can be used as part of the basis for progression in Thematic work. The next section of the book proposes a curriculum model which will bring together all of the factors which meed to be considered when planning progression and balance in thematic work throughout the primary school.

REFERENCES:

(13) Place, Time and Society 8 - 13. "Themes in Outline" (1977) Schools Council, P.13.

(14) Topic Teaching in the Primary School. Gunning, Gunning & Wilson P.33.

(15) Science in the Secondary School Curriculum.

(16) What is Happening in Our Primary Schools - H Pluckrose (1987) P.7.

(17) Teaching Information Skills through Project Work - D Wray (1987) P.31.

(18) Science in the Secondary School Curriculum.

(19) Topic Teaching in the Primary School. Gunning, Gunning& Wilson P.17.

(20) Ibid, P.20.

(21) Ibid, P.21.

(22) Starting School: An Evaluation of the Experience A.M.M.A. (1986) P.1.

23) The Early Admission to School of Four Year Old Children L.C.C. (1987) Orange P.1.

(24) Early Childhood Education. Tina Bruce (1987) Hodder & Stoughton P.3.

(25) Ibid, P.6.

(27) Ibid, P.181.

(28) The Education of Young Children. D Fontana (2nd Ed. 1984) Blackwell P.4.

(29) Early Childhood Education. Tina Bruce (1987) Hodder & Stoughton P.181.

(30) Alice Yardley in Fontana. The Ed of Young Children P.265.

(31) Early Childhood Education. Tina Bruce (1987) Hodder & Stoughton P.181.

(32) Structuring Play in the Early Years at School.

(33) With Objectives in Mind - Ennever & Harlen (1972) Macdonald Educational for the Schools Council P.60.

(34) The Popular Oxford Dictionary (1980) Oxford University Press.

(35) The Logic of Education. P.H.Hirst & R.S.Peters (1970) Rowtledge & Kegan Paul.

(36) History 5 to 9. Joan Blyth (1988) Hodder & Stoughton.

(37) Geography from 5 to 16 (1986) Curriculum Matters 7 H.M.S.O.

(38) The Periodical "Geography" Blade and Spencer "Map Use by Young Children" (1986).

(39) Primary Education in England, H.M.I. (1978) H.M.S.O.

(40) Lancashire looks at... Science in the Early Years (1986) L.C.C. P.7.

(41) Discovering an Approach (1977). Macmillan Education for Schools Council, P.11.

(42) The Westhill Project R.E. 5 - 16. G.Read J, Rudge, R.B. Howarth Mary Glasgow Publications Ltd. (1987).

(43) Design and Primary Education (1987) The Design Council, para. 3.4.

(44) The Popular Oxford Dictionary (1980) Oxford University Press.

(45) With Objectives in Mind (1972) Macdonald Ed. for Schools Council P.60.

(46) History 5 to 9. Joan Blyth (1988) Hodder & Stoughton P.29.

(47) School Without Tears. Mollie Jenkins (1973) Collins P.119

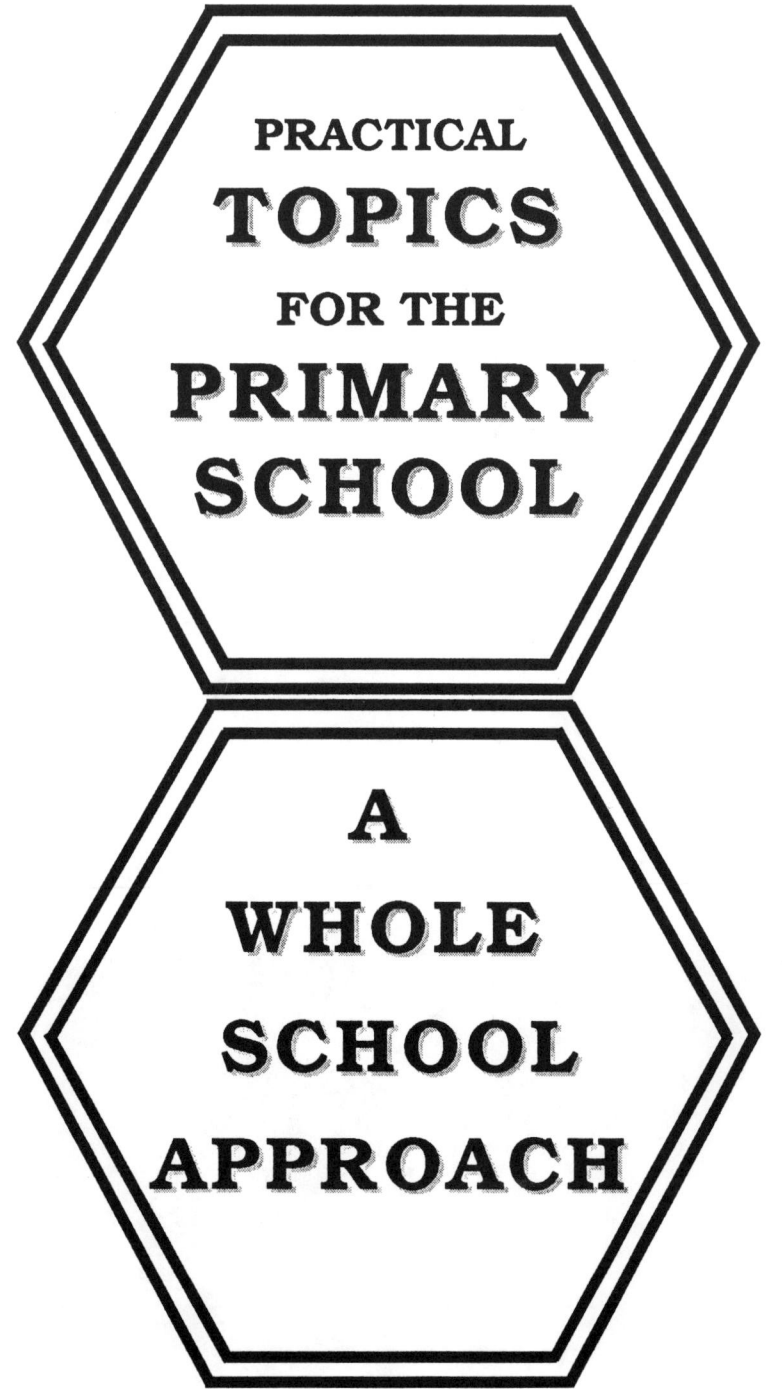

PROGRESSION

Three specific types of Topic or Theme have been identified as being appropriate to meet the demands made by the changing nature of the Primary School pupil. They are:

NURSERY/RECEPTION - THE TOTALLY CROSS-CURRICULAR THEME

For the very youngest children the bulk of the knowledge/information is new and does not need to be organised into any particular form at this stage other than to ensure that over the course of one academic year a variety of experiences have been sampled which will lay the foundations for later work in Science, Technology, History, Geography and R.E. The overiding consideration is that what is presented to be learned is of interest and is capable of catching the imagination of a pupil whose greatest concern is himself. Such Themes/Topics will be totally cross-curricular in nature and relevant to the pupils involved at that particular point in time.

INFANTS YR1/YR2 - THEMES WITH A SLIGHT BIAS TOWARDS THE:..
SCIENCES (Experimental/Nature/Technology)
HUMANITIES (History/Geography/R.E.)
TOPICAL (What is happening now)

Even at this stage subject boundaries have not yet clearly evolved and the children are still very much concerned about themselves. Themes/Topics chosen can begin to take on a slight bias towards a particular curriculum area but time still needs to be given over to work that is completely "topical". During the course of one term a "vaguely" Science Theme/Topic may be followed by a "vaguely" Humanities Theme/Topic which in turn may be followed by something purely topical and relevant to the children at that place and point in time. Such a termly pattern could be repeated three times to make up the structure for one year.

LOWER JUNIORS - THE THEME WITH A BIAS TOWARDS A DISCIPLINE

Themes/Topics carried out with lower junior aged children can last for approximately half a term and have a distinct bias towards one particular discipline (ie. Science, Nature, Technology, History, Geography or R.E.). This would give a curriculum balance over the course of one year and provide many opportunities for first hand memorable experiences and at the very least provide one part of the school year where a particular type of skill (experimenting, mapping etc.) is concentrated on and taught in some depth. In the Topic/Thematic type of approach it is inevitable that these skills will be used in other themes at other times in the year - they will occur quite naturally - but by earmarking one specific time to teach a certain type of skill in some depth will ensure they are either not missed altogether or merely skirted over several times with little understanding.

Repeating the process over the four junior years provides opportunities to return to specific skills and build upon what has gone before. In the later junior years an even more distinct bias may be given towards the subject disciplines in preparation for the transition to Secondary Schooling.

The following diagrams give examples of how the various components of Themes and Topics progress through the seven primary years.

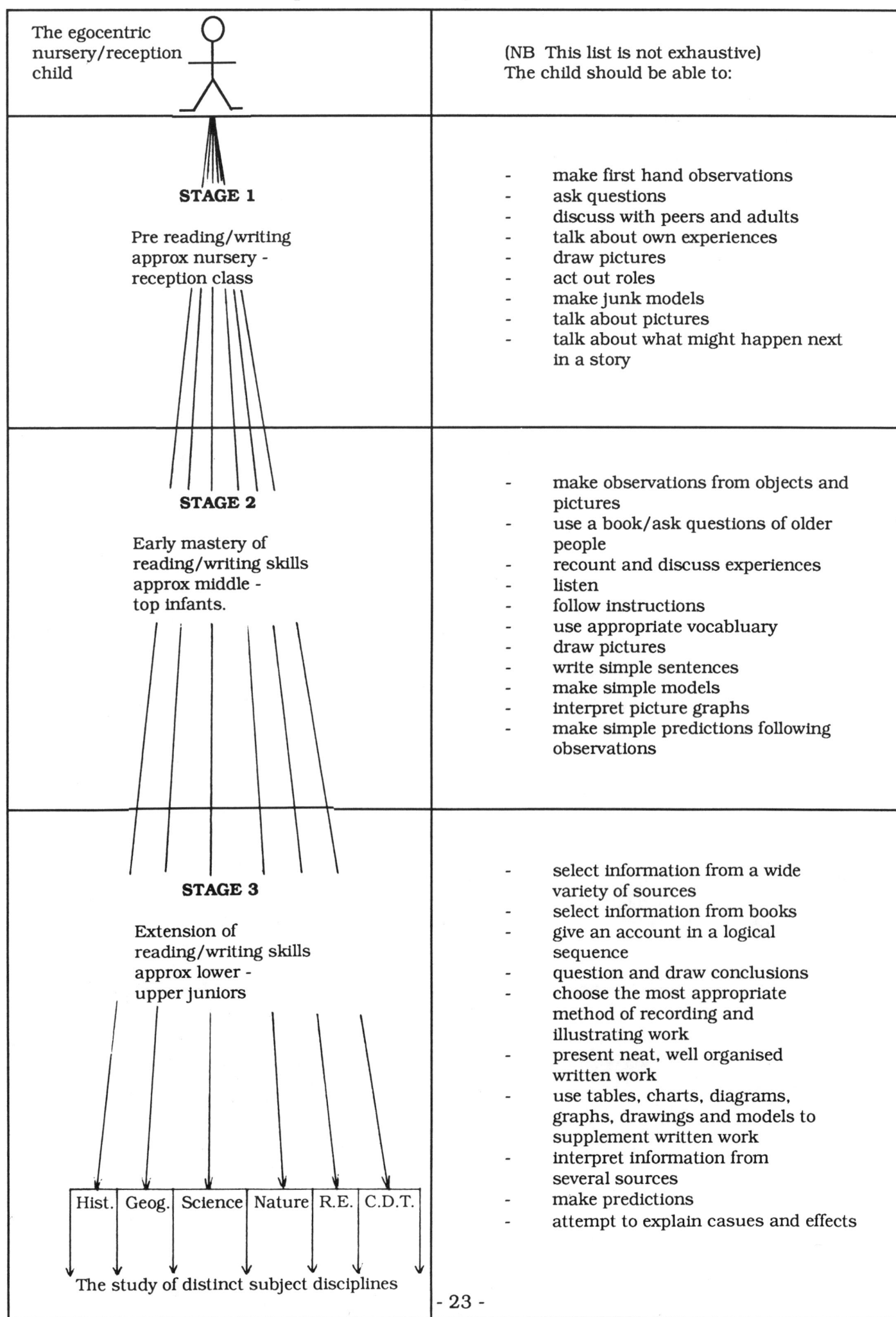

Examples of Specific Subject Skills or Characteristic Modes of Enquiry

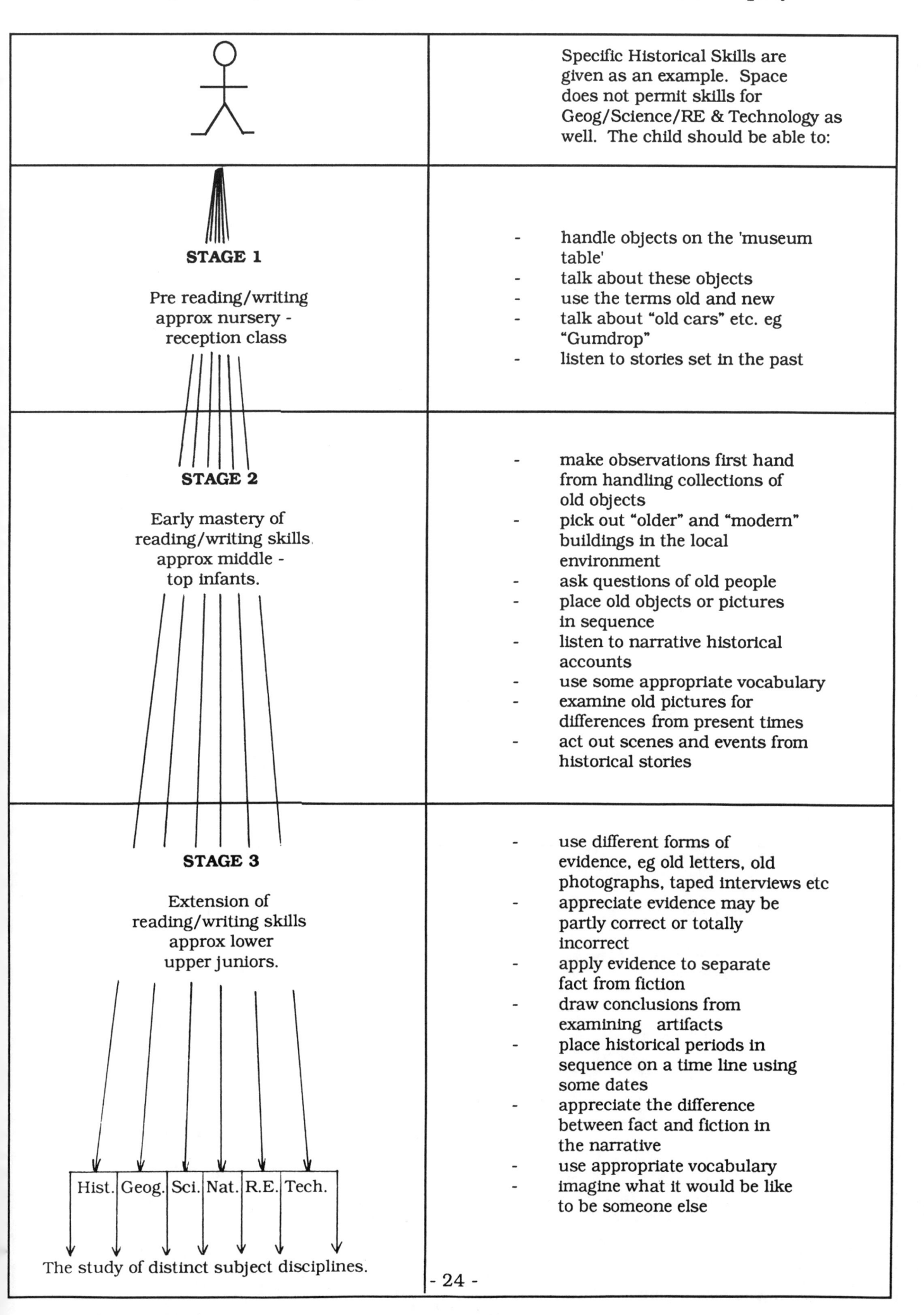

	Specific Historical Skills are given as an example. Space does not permit skills for Geog/Science/RE & Technology as well. The child should be able to:
STAGE 1 Pre reading/writing approx nursery - reception class	- handle objects on the 'museum table' - talk about these objects - use the terms old and new - talk about "old cars" etc. eg "Gumdrop" - listen to stories set in the past
STAGE 2 Early mastery of reading/writing skills approx middle - top infants.	- make observations first hand from handling collections of old objects - pick out "older" and "modern" buildings in the local environment - ask questions of old people - place old objects or pictures in sequence - listen to narrative historical accounts - use some appropriate vocabulary - examine old pictures for differences from present times - act out scenes and events from historical stories
STAGE 3 Extension of reading/writing skills approx lower upper juniors. Hist. Geog. Sci. Nat. R.E. Tech. The study of distinct subject disciplines.	- use different forms of evidence, eg old letters, old photographs, taped interviews etc - appreciate evidence may be partly correct or totally incorrect - apply evidence to separate fact from fiction - draw conclusions from examining artifacts - place historical periods in sequence on a time line using some dates - appreciate the difference between fact and fiction in the narrative - use appropriate vocabulary - imagine what it would be like to be someone else

Examples of Exploration of a Key Concept

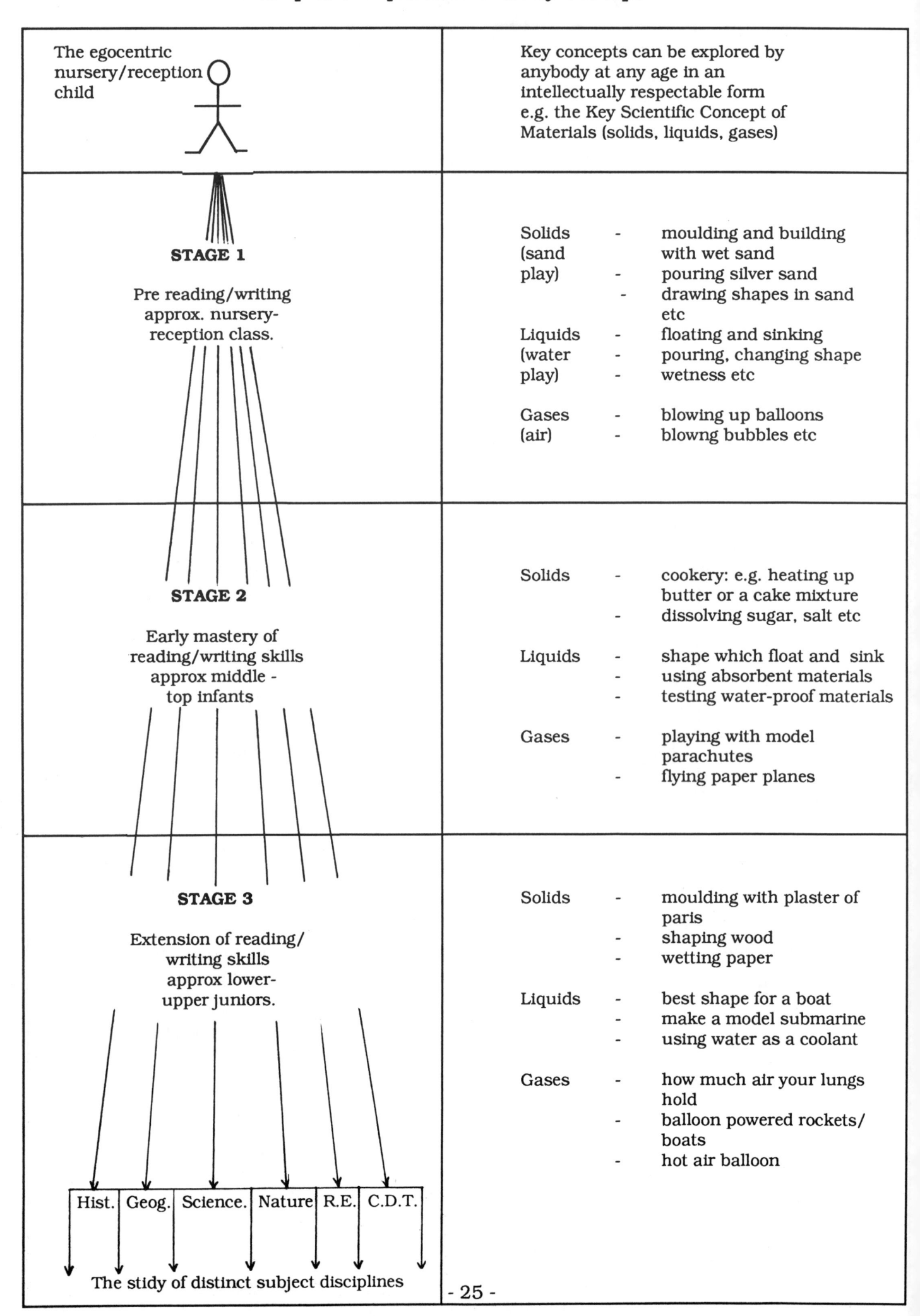

The egocentric nursery/reception child	Key concepts can be explored by anybody at any age in an intellectually respectable form e.g. the Key Scientific Concept of Materials (solids, liquids, gases)
STAGE 1 Pre reading/writing approx. nursery-reception class.	Solids (sand play) - moulding and building with wet sand - pouring silver sand - drawing shapes in sand etc Liquids (water play) - floating and sinking - pouring, changing shape - wetness etc Gases (air) - blowing up balloons - blowng bubbles etc
STAGE 2 Early mastery of reading/writing skills approx middle - top infants	Solids - cookery: e.g. heating up butter or a cake mixture - dissolving sugar, salt etc Liquids - shape which float and sink - using absorbent materials - testing water-proof materials Gases - playing with model parachutes - flying paper planes
STAGE 3 Extension of reading/writing skills approx lower-upper juniors. Hist. Geog. Science. Nature R.E. C.D.T. The stidy of distinct subject disciplines	Solids - moulding with plaster of paris - shaping wood - wetting paper Liquids - best shape for a boat - make a model submarine - using water as a coolant Gases - how much air your lungs hold - balloon powered rockets/boats - hot air balloon

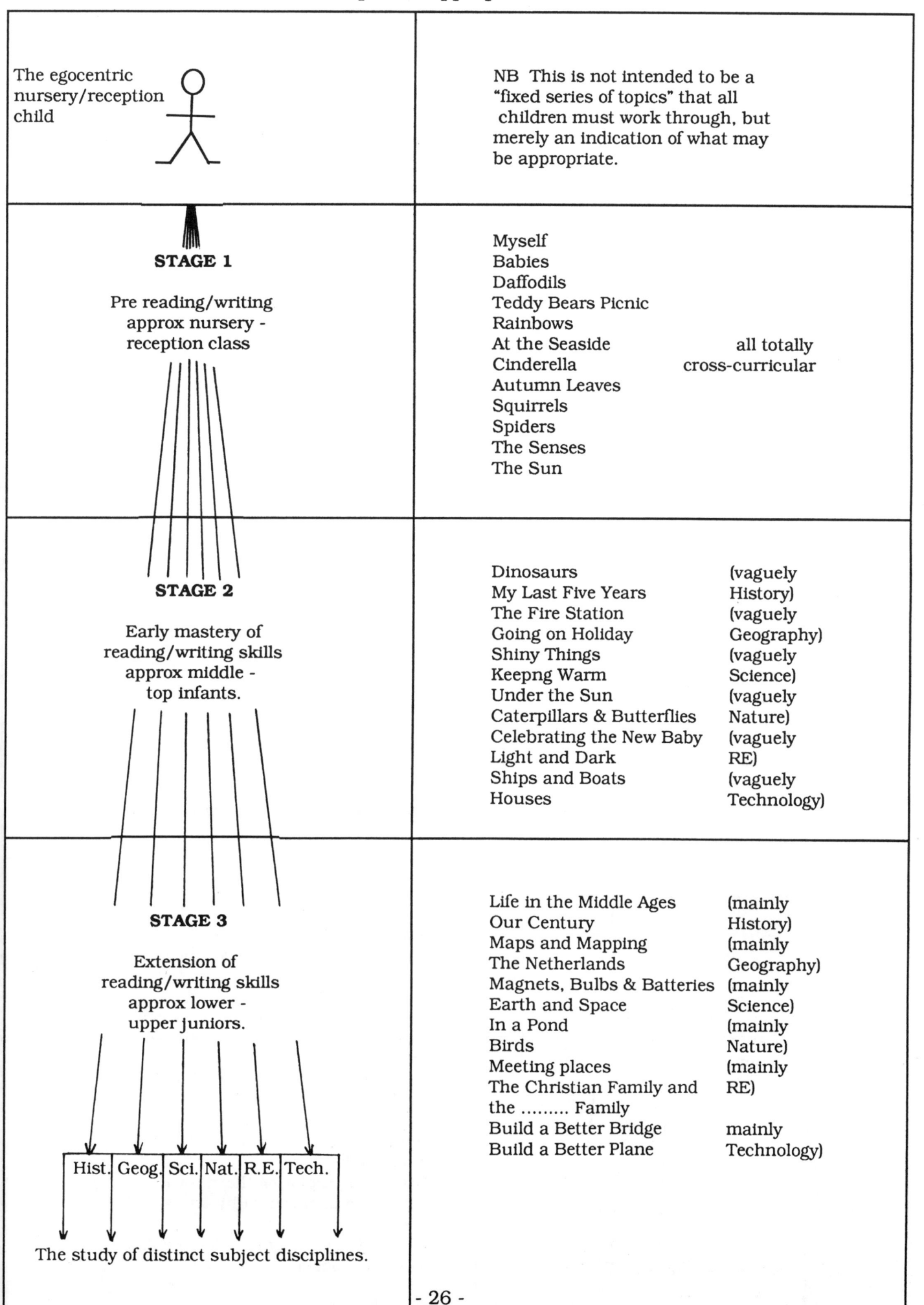

Examples of Appropriate Content

The egocentric nursery/reception child	NB This is not intended to be a "fixed series of topics" that all children must work through, but merely an indication of what may be appropriate.
STAGE 1 Pre reading/writing approx nursery - reception class	Myself Babies Daffodils Teddy Bears Picnic Rainbows At the Seaside — all totally Cinderella — cross-curricular Autumn Leaves Squirrels Spiders The Senses The Sun
STAGE 2 Early mastery of reading/writing skills approx middle - top infants.	Dinosaurs (vaguely My Last Five Years History) The Fire Station (vaguely Going on Holiday Geography) Shiny Things (vaguely Keepng Warm Science) Under the Sun (vaguely Caterpillars & Butterflies Nature) Celebrating the New Baby (vaguely Light and Dark RE) Ships and Boats (vaguely Houses Technology)
STAGE 3 Extension of reading/writing skills approx lower - upper juniors. Hist. Geog. Sci. Nat. R.E. Tech. The study of distinct subject disciplines.	Life in the Middle Ages (mainly Our Century History) Maps and Mapping (mainly The Netherlands Geography) Magnets, Bulbs & Batteries (mainly Earth and Space Science) In a Pond (mainly Birds Nature) Meeting places (mainly The Christian Family and RE) the .... Family Build a Better Bridge mainly Build a Better Plane Technology)

Examples of Appropriate Activities

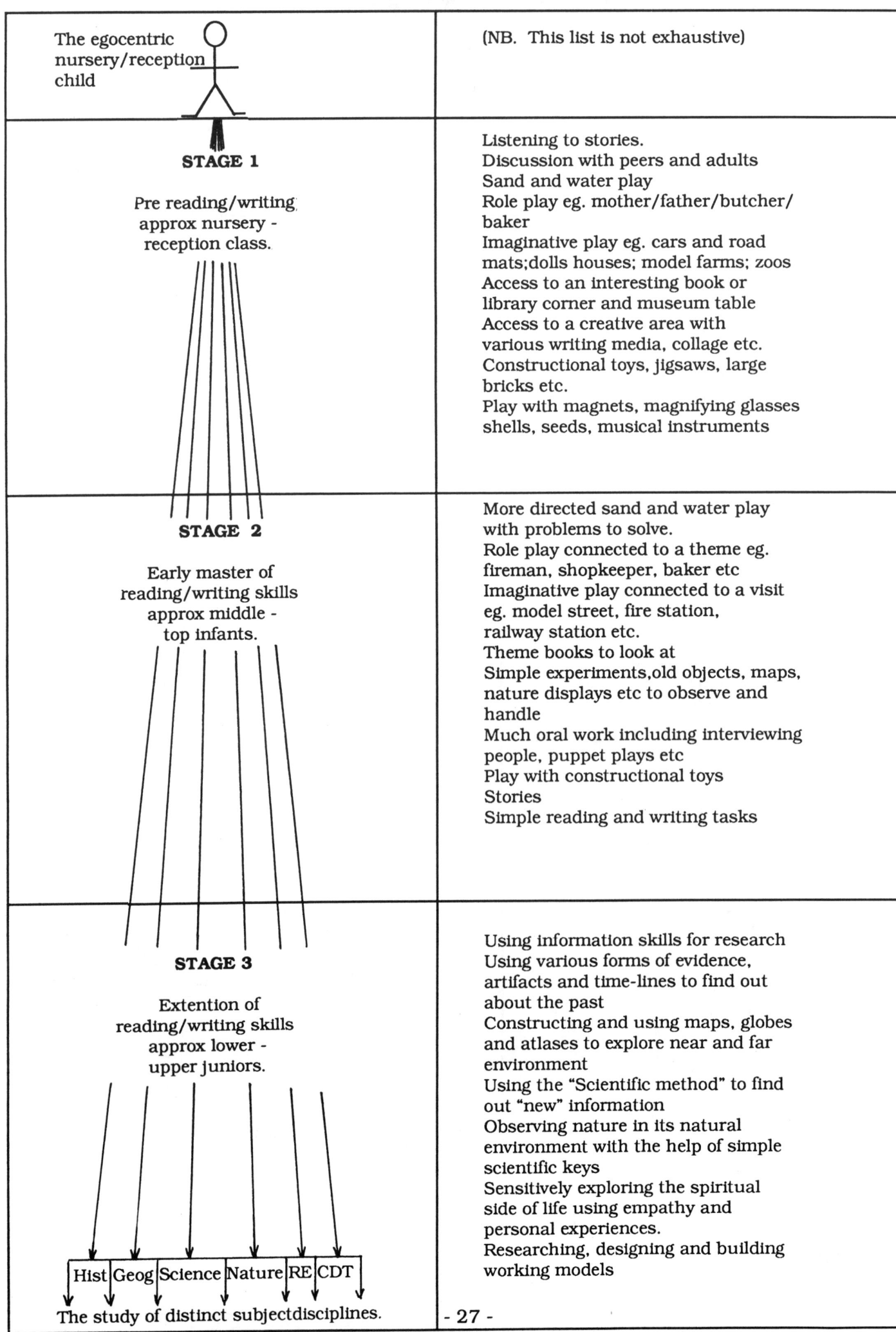

Examples of Appropriate Experiences

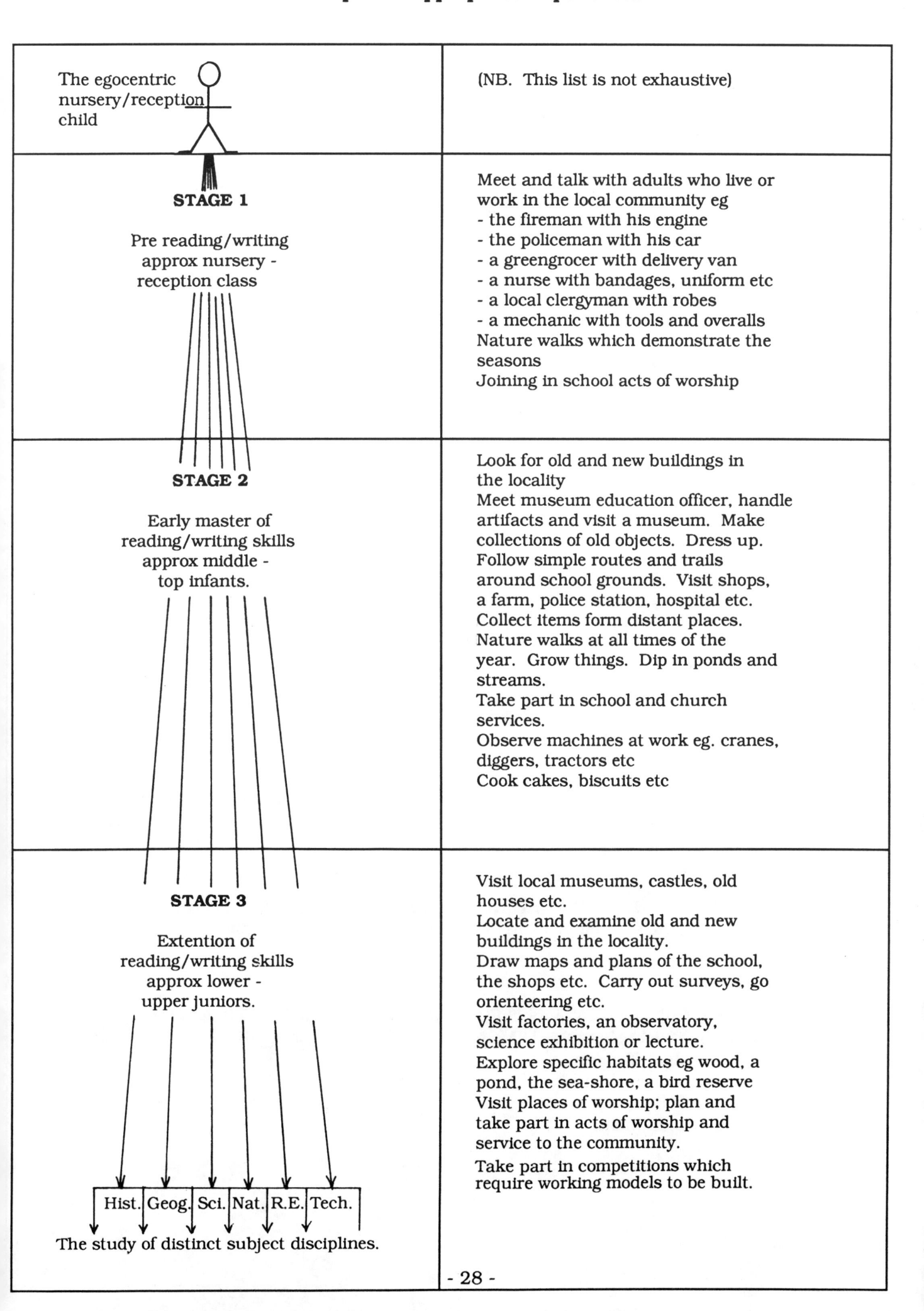

The egocentric nursery/reception child **STAGE 1** Pre reading/writing approx nursery - reception class	(NB. This list is not exhaustive) Meet and talk with adults who live or work in the local community eg - the fireman with his engine - the policeman with his car - a greengrocer with delivery van - a nurse with bandages, uniform etc - a local clergyman with robes - a mechanic with tools and overalls Nature walks which demonstrate the seasons Joining in school acts of worship
STAGE 2 Early master of reading/writing skills approx middle - top infants.	Look for old and new buildings in the locality Meet museum education officer, handle artifacts and visit a museum. Make collections of old objects. Dress up. Follow simple routes and trails around school grounds. Visit shops, a farm, police station, hospital etc. Collect items form distant places. Nature walks at all times of the year. Grow things. Dip in ponds and streams. Take part in school and church services. Observe machines at work eg. cranes, diggers, tractors etc Cook cakes, biscuits etc
STAGE 3 Extention of reading/writing skills approx lower - upper juniors. Hist. Geog. Sci. Nat. R.E. Tech. The study of distinct subject disciplines.	Visit local museums, castles, old houses etc. Locate and examine old and new buildings in the locality. Draw maps and plans of the school, the shops etc. Carry out surveys, go orienteering etc. Visit factories, an observatory, science exhibition or lecture. Explore specific habitats eg wood, a pond, the sea-shore, a bird reserve Visit places of worship; plan and take part in acts of worship and service to the community. Take part in competitions which require working models to be built.

BALANCE

Specific subject disciplines have been identified in the National Curriculum as being essential to form a curriculum which is balanced and broadly based. In a Primary School they include English, Mathematics, Science, Technology, History, Geography, Art, Music, PE. as well as RE. A Topic/Thematic approach can be balanced over the course of one year (instead of the more common weekly or even termly balance) by considering the bias towards subject disciplines within the Topics carried out in any one academic year, as shown in the opposite diagram:

NB The diagram considers Science, Technology, History, Geography and RE only.

THE NATIONAL CURRICULUM   During the 1990's ....

BASIC STUDY AND INFORMATION SKILLS will be dictated by the English National Curriculum.

SPECIFIC SUBJECT SKILLS will be dictated by the individual National Curriculum documents in Science, Technology, History and Geography. The S.A.C.R.E.'s will provide information on the specific skills to be developed in RE.

The **CONCEPTS** to be explored will be dictated mainly by the content or subject material to be covered.

The **CONTENT** will be dictated by the Programmes of study found in the individual National Curriculum documents for Science, Technology, History and Goeraphy. The S.A.C.R.E.'s will provide information on the content to be developed in RE.

Appropriate **ACTIVITIES** and **EXPERIENCES** will be provided by the schools and in particular by the individual class teachers in their day to day work of delivering the National Curriculum.

The National Curriculum documents contain **ATTAINMENT TARGETS** which in turn are broken down into **LEVELS OF ATTAINMENT** usually on a scale of 1 - 10. If a teacher covers the appropriate content (Programmes of Study) and teaches the relevant skills the outcome will be measured from time to time and recorded for each individual pupil by stating the level of attainment reached in individual Attainment Targets or groups of Attainment Targets known as Profile Components.

BALANCING THEMES/TOPICS OVER THE COURSE OF ONE SCHOOL YEAR

←──────────────── One academic year ────────────────→

RECEPTION	A variety of short (2 or 3 weeks) themes which reflect the interests of the children over one school year may touch on elements of Science, Nature, Technology, History, Geography and R.E.

INFANTS YRS 1 & 2

Vaguely Science	Vaguely Humanities	Completely Topical	Vaguely Humanities	Completely Topical	Vaguely Science	Completely Topical	Vaguely Science	Vaguely Humanities
Vaguely Humanities	Completely Topical	Vaguely Science	Completely Topical	Vaguely Humanities	Vaguely Science	Vaguely Science	Vaguely Humanities	Completely Topical

LOWER JUNIORS YRS 3 & 4

Practical Science Bias	History Bias	Technology Bias	Geography Bias	Natural Science Bias	R.E. Bias
Gegraphy Bias	Practical Science Bias	History Bias	Technology Bias	R.E. Bias	Natural Science Bias

UPPER JUNIORS YRS 5 & 6

Definite Practical Science Bias	Definite History Bias	Definite Technology Bias	Definite Geography Bias	Definite Natural Science Bias	Definite R.E. Bias
Definite History Bias	Definite Technology Bias	Definite R.E. Bias	Definite Practical Science Bias	Definite Geography Bias	Definite Natural Science Bias

←── **AUTUMN TERM** ──→ ←── **SPRING TERM** ──→ ←── **SUMMER TERM** ──→

Infants, Lower Juniors and Upper Juniors could work on a two year rolling cycle for variety.

IN CONCLUSION

A WHOLE SCHOOL THEMATIC APPROACH WHICH WILL DELIVER THE NATIONAL CURRICULUM IN SCIENCE, TECHNOLOGY, HISTORY, GEOGRAPHY AND R.E.

A whole school approach can be constructed by combining:

(A) The three different types of Topic/Theme which cover the seven primary years.

(B) Themes chosen with a bias towards a number of curriculum areas to provide a balanced curriculum over the course of any one academic year.

(C) Themes that are constructed from Programmes of Study and the Specific Skills identified by the National Curriculum Documents.

The rest of this book will be concerned with the practicalities of putting into the classroom a programme of Themes/Topics that will cover the content (Programmes of Study) of the National Curriculum and provide opportunities to teach and use the skills necessary for pupils to work towards the appropriate Attainment Targets.

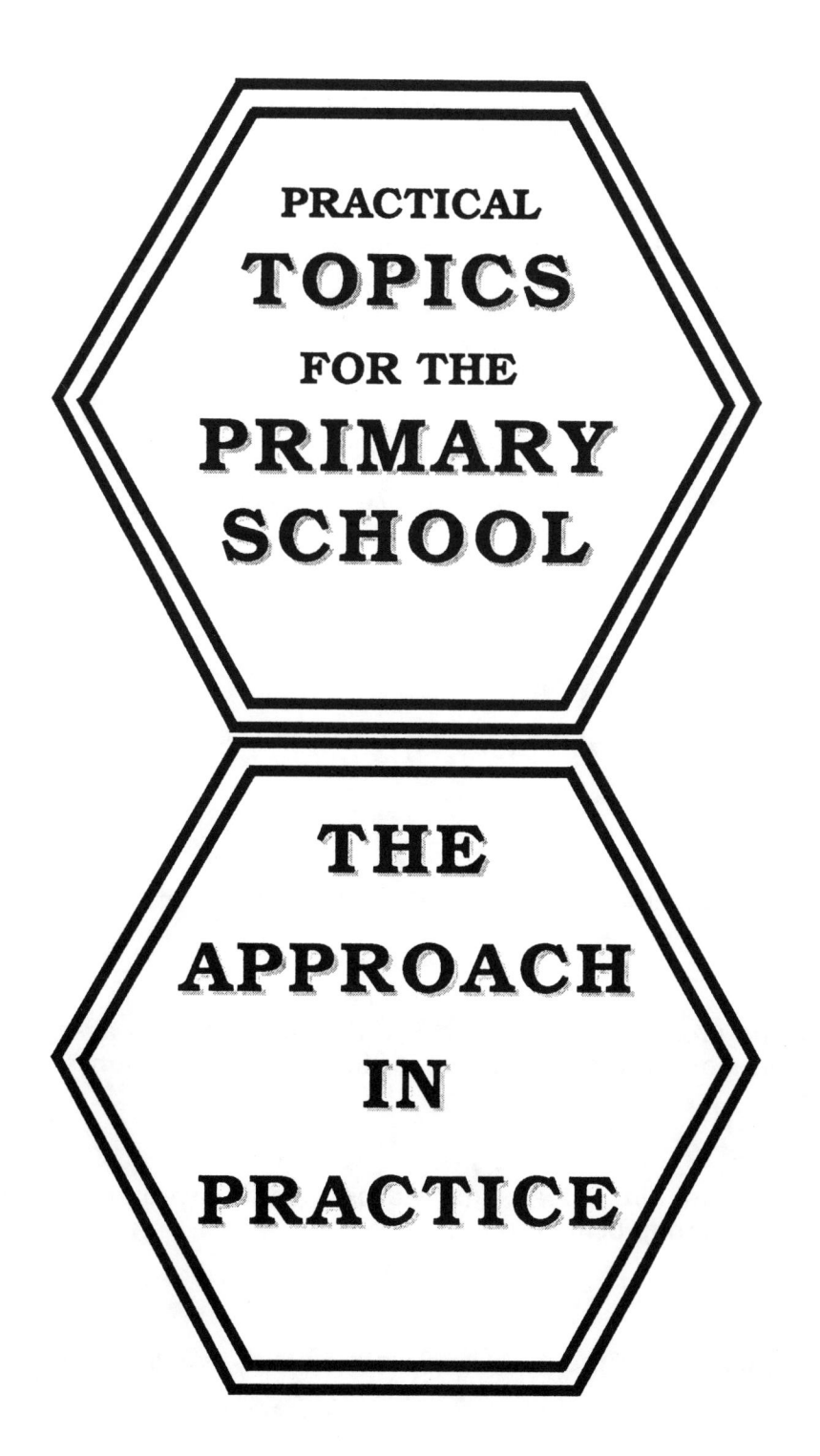

PRACTICAL TOPICS FOR THE PRIMARY SCHOOL

THE APPROACH IN PRACTICE

PLANNING A TOPIC

Some time before a Topic takes place the teacher will ....

(1) Decide which area of knowledge she/he wishes to develop ie. History, Geography, Science, Nature, R.E., Technology.

(2) Decide on a name of central theme.

(3) Decide on the programme of study she/he wants the children to explore.

(4) Decide on the skills she/he wants the children to develop.

(5) Devise activities that will help the children practise these skills and encounter the programme of study.

(6) Decide on a possible method of organising the children's work.

(7) Decide on the end product required, e.g. a wall display, a class assembly or presentation, class or individual booklets, radio or T.V. programmes etc.

(8) Collect books, posters, film strips, slides videos, computer programmes etc, suitable for the age group being taught.

(9) Investigate the possiblity of a suitable, relevant educational visit or guest speaker.

(To aid this process a Topic Planning Sheet may be filled in - see appendix 3).

CARRYING OUT A TOPIC

The teacher will ....

(1) Introduce the Topic in as lively or stimulating way as possible to create interest.

(2) Organise the children into working on the various activities, putting right any problems of ability match or lack of resources as they arise.

(3) Help the children discover information, oversee the organisation of group or individual work and to see that each child has a suitable amount of work for its capability.

(4) Encourage individual children to develop ideas of their own connected with the topic over and above the provision make in school.

(5) Visit the place to be explored and plan a day's activities.

(6) Book a coach, date for the visit, time set., collect in money, remind about sandwiches, suitable clothing etc, inform the kitchen that 30? children will be away for the day.

(7) Devise activities to follow up the visit.

(8) Finish off the work in some way so that the children can see that they have achieved something worthwhile eg. a 3D model or display; oral presentation; a booklet which they can keep as a reminder afterwards.

(9) Look back at the Topic as a whole and try to assess if she/he has managed to achieve exactly what she/he set out to achieve.

(To aid this process an Assessment Sheet and Topic Questionaire may be filled in - see appendix 4.)

SOME PRACTICAL CONSIDERATIONS

(A) Organisation of Written Work

When doing projects and subsequently gathering lots of new information it is very useful for the children to compile their own topic "folder" or "booklet". This has several advantages over using an exercise book. eg.

(1) Children can take great pride if they know that they will keep the finished product.

(2) Making a folder rather than writing in just "another" exercise book makes the topic just a little bit different from ordinary Maths or English work.

(3) A child who has taken great care over a particular topic may request to repeat a sub-standard piece of work and this is more easily carried out with the poor piece of work removed when using a folder.

(4) Similarly, the teacher can request individual pieces of work to be improved.

(5) A folder provides plenty of opportunity for expansion for those pupils who wish to do extra work at home.

(6) A new topic and hence new folder provides a fresh start for those children who felt they didn't do as well as they could have in their previous work.

(7) Duplicated information sheets printed by the teacher on A4 paper can easily be included in the folder.

(8) When the topic is completed it is an easy matter to remove "good" pieces of work for a class display (rather than copying out again).
It is important however, to make sure that the displayed piece of work is returned to the folder when the display is discarded.

(9) Single items of work may be removed to use in group or class discussion providing opportunities for the development of listening and speaking skills.

A good way of collecting well presented and corrected topic work for inclusion in the finished folder is to:

(i) Allow the children if they want to, or are poor writers or spellers, to do a rough copy first. (I often do this with everyone in class when introducing topic work, gradually working towards as many as possible doing a neat copy at the first attempt.)

(ii) After the rough copy has been corrected, allow the children to copy up the work on A4 size duplicating paper. This looks attractive if a 1 cm border is drawn round the outside of the page.

(iii) Finally, draw in any pictures. If each child has a set of lines to rest on,(see example in Appendix 7) the neat copy will have evenly spaced horizontal writing and and appropriate spaces may be left in the text for the inclusion of pictures.e.g.

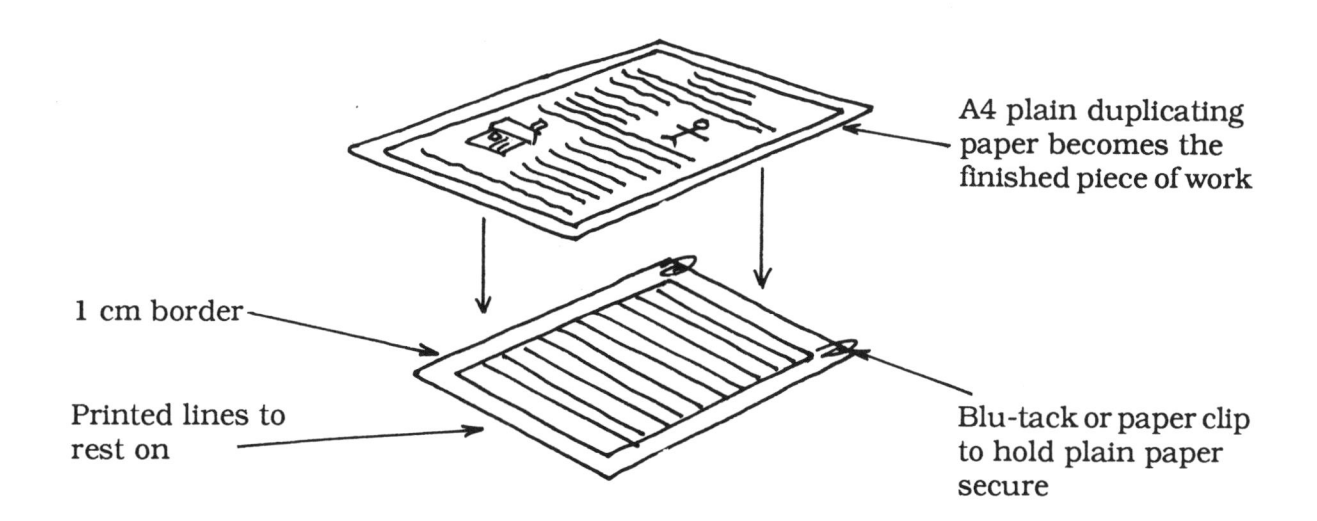

A4 plain duplicating paper becomes the finished piece of work

1 cm border

Printed lines to rest on

Blu-tack or paper clip to hold plain paper secure

The finished pieces of work are collected together throughout the term of the project in a manilla folder. Finally an appropriate cover is made and all the pages stapled together.

(An example of a set of lines to use underneath plain paper can be found in Appendix 7.)

(B) **Lack of Expertise!**
Some teachers are often afraid to tackle a project in an area where they themselves have not a lot of expertise. Whereas the author agrees that they will probably make a better job in the area they are more familiar with, if for no other reason than they have more confidence in that area, this should not be used as an excuse for not tackling the less familiar. If for example, a Geography student was required to tackle a Science project say on Electricity or a History project on Henry VIII all she/he would have to do is read beforehand an appropriate book eg. Magnets and Electricity by Ladybird and this would provide 95% of the answers to questions she/he may be asked. The other 5% could be dealt with as problem solving activities and hence would encourage children's research.

(C) **Mixed Ability Teaching**
The area in which doing a topic scores best over the whole class working from a set book is in the opportunities available for children to work at a level suitable for their own ability. Every teacher knows that a class has bright, average and poor children so the majority of the activities included in one particular topic should cater for at least three different levels of ability. This does not mean that class teaching should not be encouraged. Indeed, it is very valuable at such times as introducing a new topic, getting together to point out a common mistake or as a way of drawing together and finishing off.

(D) **Library and Museum Loans**
Local authorities generally have provision for schools to borrow a "project loan" from the library service and "artifacts" from a museum loans service. To make good use of these services items often need to be booked some time before they are required.

(E) **Two age groups in one class**

This chart shows one way a school can avoid repeating Topic Work when two age groups are present in each Junior class.

(Each class works on a two year cycle.)

	First Year of Cycle	Second Year of Cycle
Lower Junior Class	BAND 1 TOPICS	BAND 2 TOPICS
Middle Junior Class	BAND 3 TOPICS	BAND 2 TOPICS
Upper Junior Class	BAND 3 TOPICS	BAND 4 TOPICS

If three age groups are present in one class, or Infants are present in the Lower Junior Class, or a teacher has a preference for a particular area of study it may be more appropriate or necessary to choose an alternative History, Geography, Science Technology, Nature or R.E. Topic.

As long as the appropriate **skills** and programme of study are developed and this **work is not repeated** in another junior age group this is perfectly acceptable. The only drawback is that the school may not be as well resourced for an area of study outside the recognized scheme.

(F) **Grouping of Pupils**

There is no ideal way of organising "30" children to work in one room with one adult. I find there is a time for whole class teaching, small group work and individual activity. The following notes taken from "Classroom Organisation for Primary Science" by Simon Naison may give some food for thought.

Single Group For Class Teaching

Advantages
(1) Maximum interaction with teacher.
(2) Good input of information and ideas.
(3) Many teachers find it easiest.

Disadvantages
(1) Less opportunity for development of skills.
(2) Difficult to allow for abilities and interests.
(3) Can make heavy demands on resources.

Individual Enquiry

Advantages
(1) Development of enquiry skils.
(2) Children able to pursue own interests.
(3) Allows children to work at own level.
Disadvantages
(1) Lack of depth and understanding perhaps.
(2) Much practical work not viable purely on grounds of the amount of equipment and materials needed.
(3) Lack of interchange of ideas between children.

Small Groups with Identical Assignments

Advantages
(1) Easy comparison of measurements and observations.
(2) Good control of teacher planned activities.
(3) Easy for recording/assessment purposes.
Disadvantages
(1) Uneconomical use of resources.
(2) Narrow range of interest in classroom.
(3) Space limitations.

Small Group Rotating through a Series of Assignments

Advantages
(1) All pupils eventually cover same ground.
(2) Resources can be managed in very systematic way.
(3) Generally seems to stimulate interest.
Disadvantages
(1) Little scope for extending children's own ideas.
(2) Assumes equal time required for all assignments and all groups.
(3) Places additional loads on the teacher interms of keeping track of progress in each assignment.
(4) Cannot sequence experiences for best effect.

Small Groups Pursuing Different but Related Assignments

Advantages
(1) Activities contributing to class interest or topic.
(2) Groups able to pursue aspect of topic to some depth.
(3) Can be economical in resources.
Disadvantages
(1) Less structured and requiring greater teacher confidence.
(2) Greater chance of unproductive effort leading to "blind alley".
(3) The load on the teacher is greater than in the above.
(4) Less able may find it disheartening.

Small Groups with Different Topics

Advantages
(1) Scope for study in depth and experiment design.
(2) Motivation provided by group interests and identity.

(3) Can make good use of resources.

Disadvantages
(1) Lacks dimension of co-operative class achievement.
(2) Harder to maintain progressive structure of content.
(3) The load on the teacher in terms of keeping track of each group and each topic is at a maximum.
(4) Constant cross reporting between groups is needed.
(5) Less able quite unaware of what others are doing.

(G) Organisation of Resources

If a school decides to adopt a Whole School Thematic Approach to the National Curriculum with relatively "fixed" themes or topics then resources can be systematically purchased and stored until they are required eg:

Posters
A poster bank may be built up using existing resources and planned purchases. A poster pack (eg. 8/10 posters on a similar theme) would be borrowed by a teacher for the duration of their topic and returned to the central bank after use.

Slides/Videos
Appropriate slides/videos may be recorded or purchased to fit in with chosen themes and kept in a central resource. Care must be taken not to infringe copyright.

School Library
Once a selection of 40 or so different topics have been agreed upon the school library can be checked to ensure it has a range of books to cover each theme.

School Museum
If space allows, artifacts could be donated from the local community to help with History work. I know of one primary school that used the local radio station to help them do this.

Core Book
It is extremely useful when working on a theme, (eg. Electricity & Magnetism) to have multiple copies of one simple "core" book. Sets of 10 (approx 1 between 3) or 15 (approx 1 between 2) may be purchased and stored centrally.

Technology Resources
A trolley (or two) containing small hand tools and specialized building materials (eg. balsa wood/corriflute) could be purchased and wheeled into the class working on a "Technology" theme or topic. When this work is finished, the tools and resources would be wheeled to another class working on C.D.T.

Computer Programmes
Word Processing, Data Base, Graphics, Simulations, Control Technology and Concept Keyboard programmes can also be purchased to fit in to particular topics.

(H) **ASSESSMENT**

There seems little point in making elaborate plans for assessment until Central Government have made definite decisions about the form National Curriculum Assessment is to take. However, one simple approach would be to test how effective a particular topic, which is currently in progress, is in developing specified skills and exploring relevant programmes of strudy by using a chart such as this: ....

- ✓ = can perform the skill/understands the content
- x = cannot perform the skill/does not understand the content
- ? = not easy to judge

TOPIC TITLE / Name of Child	Examples of Programme of Study (content)	Skills to be developed

The chart could be filled in during "quiet moments" whilst the children were working on various activities and the teacher was wandering around the class.

If it was felt too time consuming to observe closely every child in the class during each activity then similar results could be obtained by observing only one or two bright children, three or four average children and one or two poor children.

Looking horizontally across the chart gives an indication of individual or ability group progress whilst working on that topic.

Looking vertically at the chart gives an indication of how effective the set activities have been in developing the required skills and programme of study. This information can then be used to help modify and improve the pupil activities.

This, plus a short questionnaire for the teacher to fill in, would give a good indication of how successful a particular project had been.

(See Appendix 4 for an example of such an assessment sheet).

PRACTICAL TOPICS FOR THE PRIMARY SCHOOL

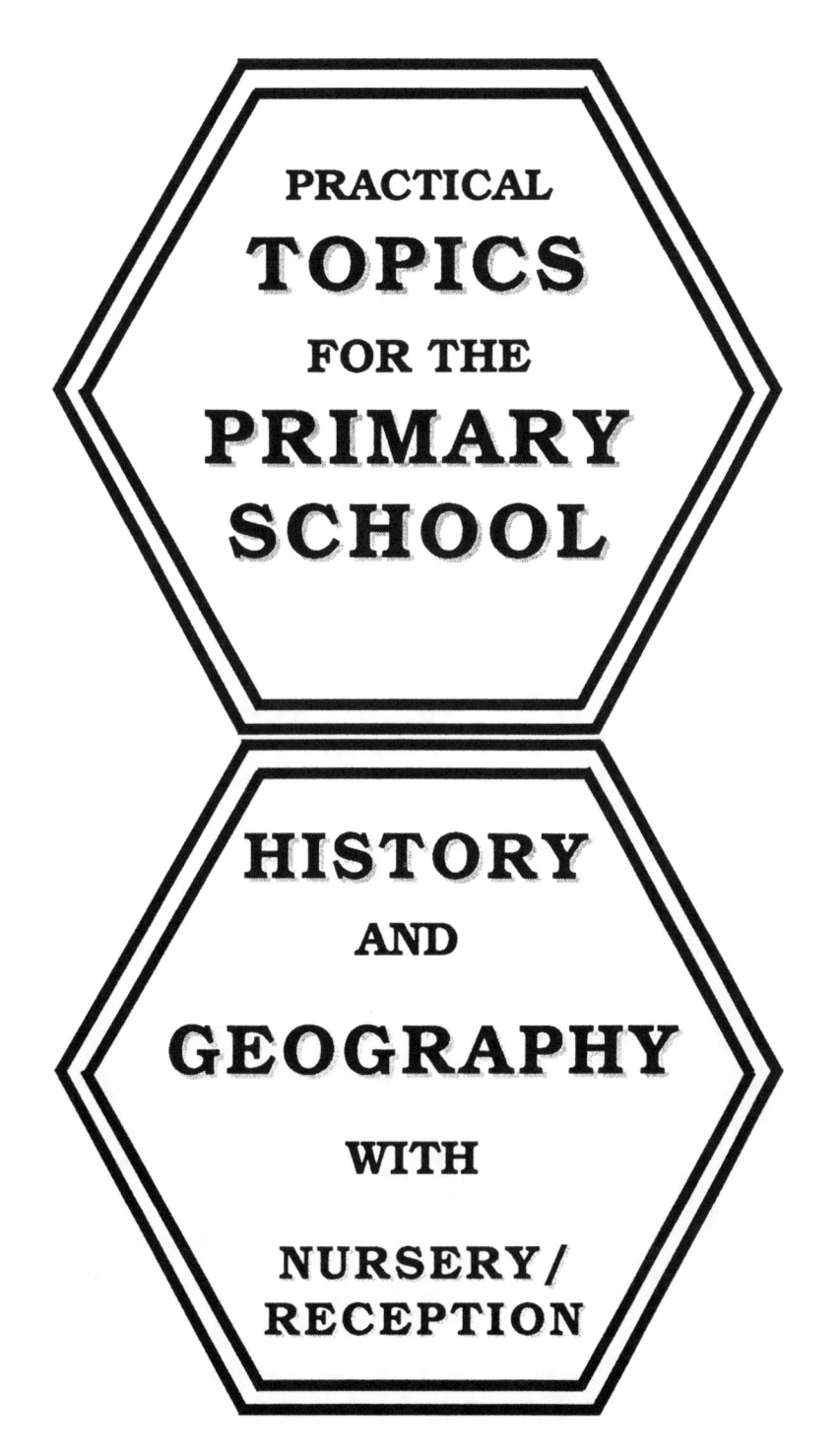

HISTORY AND GEOGRAPHY WITH NURSERY/RECEPTION

HISTORY AND GEOGRAPHY WITH NURSERY/RECEPTION

There are 4 aspects to this work:

(1) On - Going Activities
Weather recording, random nature walks, free play with road mats, model farms, dolls houses, model railway sets, the home corner, the shop, constructing with bricks, dressing up etc. Free play with sand and water. Details of activities which may be included in "an appropriate learning environment which provides much practical experience" can be found on the next page.

(2) The Museum Table/Far Away Table (or Interest Table)
These tables should provide opportunities for discussion and hands on experience of: old every day household items e.g. flat iron, shoe last, poker, old photographs, bottles and jars etc or objects brought back from distant places such as produce packaging, photographs, post cards, souvenirs etc (although care must be taken not to portray stereo-types). Regular change of displays will provide on going interest in the table/tables.

(3) Short Cross - Curricular Themes
These themes may last two or three weeks and must be relevant to the pupils involved at that particular point in time. Four detailed examples are given (Winter, The Cafe, Homes, Spring) Experienced teachers will know of many more alternatives.

(4) Information Technology (Computer Studies)
Pupils should have the opportunity to:
(a) Experience control of lights, T.V.'s, radios, tape recorders, cookers, telephones etc.
(b) Play with toys which can be programmed.
(c) Use a concept key-board to operate a computer.

OUTDOOR PLAY EQUIPMENT

Examples could be:
a slide
a climbing frame
ride on toys
trolleys/carts
a swing etc.

SAND PLAY EQUIPMENT

e.g.
wet sand
dry sand
rakes
spades
scoops etc.

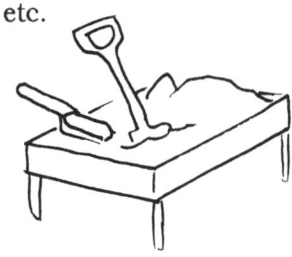

WATER PLAY

e.g.
water tray
coloured water
sponge
corks
boats
watering can
various containers
various pourers
things that float
things that sink
syringes
droppers
toy pump

BOOK/LIBRARY CORNER

e.g.
books
posters
photograph albums
magazines etc.

Computer

With concept keyboard and appropriate software.

CREATIVE AREA

e.g.
paper
paint
collage materials
scissors
pieces of card
junk modelling materials etc.

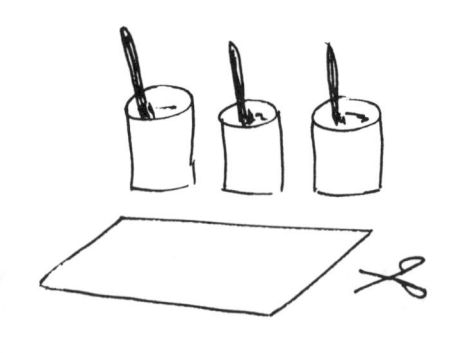

NURS
RECEP
ENVIRO

"An appropriate learn
which provides much

SCIENCE TABLE

Examples of practical things to try out could include:
batteries
bulbs
wires
crocodile clips
model lighthouse etc.

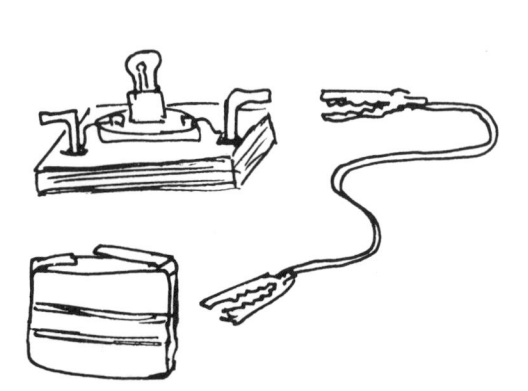

NATURE TABLE

Examples of collections appropriate to the season could include:
daffodils
bulbs
pussywillow
posters etc.

MUSIC

e.g.
drums
triangles
tambourines
stringed instruments
tape recorder etc

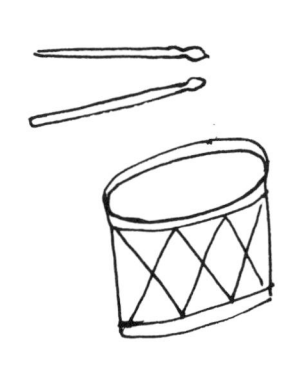

EQUIPMENT

funnels and tubes
different shaped containers
spoons
whisks
polystyrene tiles
sieve
washing up liquid
bottles
pieces of wood
kitchen spatulas
various funnels etc.

HOME CORNER EQUIPMENT

e.g.
table
chairs
sink
dolls bed
table
mirror
fireplace
telephone
writing pads etc.

IMAGINATIVE PLAY EQUIPMENT

e.g.
farm
dressing up clothes
puppets
train set
dolls house
large jigsaws
bricks
road mat and cars etc.

ERY/ TION NMENT

ing environment
practical experience".

TABLE APPARATUS

e.g.
constructional toys such as
Brio or Duplo (Technology)
jigsaws
fuzzy felts
dominos etc.

WRITING TABLE

e.g.
note pads
coloured paper
shaped paper
various writing materials
including pencils, crayons,
felt tips
stapler
hole puncher etc.

TABLE

Homemade instruments
e.g.
shakers
yoghurt cartons
bottles of water
elastic band pluckers
cardboard box thumpers
sandpaper blocks
hung nail chimers
wooden spoon rhythm

MUSEUM TABLE

Examples of old objects to
examine and talk about
could include:
old photographs
old bottles and jars
shoe last
boiler hat
spectacles
camera
fossils etc.

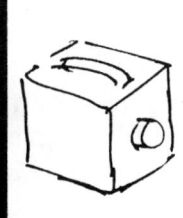

FAR AWAY TABLE

Examples of artifacts from
distant countries could include:
sweet wrappers
dolls
ornaments
examples of dress
post cards
pictures etc.

Alongside "an appropriate learning environment which provides much practical experience" may run a totally cross-curricular theme such as:

WINTER

Language: Collect words to describe cold, howling winds - wet muddy weather - feelings of being stuck inside. Contrast with a snowy day (First hand experience of one is best!) - light, bright flakes, - white carpet - everything looks new, clean - crisp and soft. Walk in fresh snow, make footprints, throw snowballs etc. Listen to wintry stories such as "Postman Pat Goes Sledging".

Maths: Make sets of six snowmen, seven winter trees, eight Father Christmas' etc. Measure out ingredients to make ice lollies. Sort winter twigs into heavier/lighter or fatter/thinner sets.

Science & Technology: Fill a jar with snow and watch it melt - what does it turn into? Has it shrunk? Half fill a plastic bottle with water and place inside a freezer. How does it change? How long does it take to melt? Do you end up with more or less water? Make umbrellas using different materials - which is best at keeping people dry? How can we test it? How can we improve the umbrella?

Humanities: Get wrapped up and go for a walk in the school grounds/local environment. Talk about directions left and right. Observe how fresh snow makes buildings look different. Why do trees look different in winter? How do people dress to keep warm? What happens to traffic on snowy days? Listen to stories about Father Christmas. How is Christmas celebrated in other lands, if at all?

R.E.: The Christmas story. Birth stories from other faiths. Consider who needs special care in Winter time? How do people look after their pets e.g. rabbits, guinea pigs etc. What special care do old people need? Who gets them their shopping, tidies garden etc.

Music: Listen to music which suggests cold wintry weather. Listen to a sound/video tape of the snowman by Raymond Briggs.

P.E./Movement/Drama: Move with the weather's moods: calm slow movements; fast whirling movements; gentle falling snow; fierce biting winds etc.

Art & Craft: Make a snowy frieze. Make a collage snowman, children sledging, throwing snowballs, snow covered buildings, scarecrow etc. Use block prints to make repeating patterns of falling snow. Cut out snow flakes from folded paper. Make silhouettes of bare trees. Make model snowmen.

Alongside "an appropriate learning environment which provides much practical experience" may run a totally cross curricular theme such as:

HOMES

Language: Listen to the story of the "Three Little Pigs" Ladybird; or "Topsy & Tim Move House" by J. & G. Adamson - Pub. Blackie. Talk about types of houses, e.g. semi-detached - terraced etc. Talk about the names of rooms e.g. lounge, sitting room, dining room, living room, kitchen etc. What are they all used for? Talk about animal homes, burrows, nests, caves etc.

Maths: Draw rows of houses and put numbers on the doors. Count the windows, doors, chimneys etc on a house. Count chicks in a nest, pigs in a sty etc. Sort animals into the correct type of home.

Science & Technology: Talk about materials houses are made of. Make a display of building materials. What were the "Three Little Pigs" houses made of? Which was the best house? Why? Make models of them. Build houses with different constructions e.g. Lego, wooden bricks, cardboard boxes etc.

Humanities: Go for a walk in the local environment. Look for different types of houses. Make rubbings of bricks and other materials. Make a simple map of the route you took. Make a map of the route taken by the Wolf in the Three Little Pigs. Look at pictures and talk about houses of long ago.

R.E.: What makes a house a home? In a home you feel warm, dry, well fed and safe - there are people to look after you. Who looked after Jesus when he was young? What sort of home did he have?

Music: This Little Puffin - compiled by Elizabeth Matterson - Pub. by Puffin Books - a section of this book is devoted to "In the House".

P.E./Movement/Drama: Act out the construction of a house or the story of The Three Little Pigs. Make bird/animal movements building houses - see "Birds and Animals" in This Little Puffin.

Art & Craft: Make junk models of house, flats, bungalows etc. Make a frieze/collage of different animal houses e.g. rabbit in burrow, bird in nest etc. Make bird nests from hay and place eggs inside. Print brick patterns to make a wall - Make clay plaques of houses.

Alongside "an appropriate learning environment which provides much practical experience" may run a totally cross curricular theme such as:

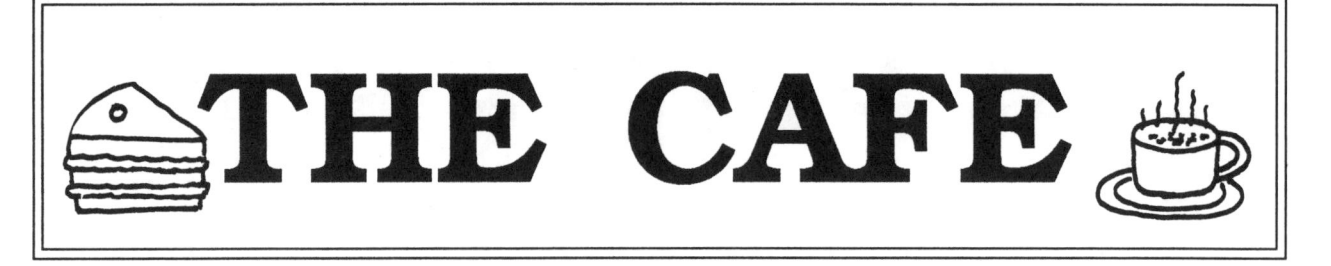

THE CAFE

Language: Talk about eating out - Who has been? - Where did they go? - Why? What did they have to eat? Listen to the story of "Mrs Wobble the Waitress" by A. & J. Ahlberg Pub. Puffin/Viking Kestrel. Talk about setting up your own CAFE. What would you need? Food, tables, chairs, menus, waiters, cash till etc.

Maths: Number rhymes which include food (see music). Count cakes, buns, biscuits etc. Sort foods into sets. Weigh ingredients for baking. Price cakes and use money and till to buy. Take orders for meals and drinks.

Science & Technology: Talk about how foods change when they are cooked. Set a jelly. Make chocolate crispy cakes. Talk about different types of tastes and hold a tasting competition. Plan a party in the cafe.

Humanities: Set up your cafe in an appropriate place. Set out tables and chairs, a counter, a till etc. Make simple plans of the cafe. Talk about where we get different kinds of food from. Look at pictures of long ago. Did they have cafes then?

R.E.: Make up or learn sime simple graces. Why do some people say these? Talk about harvest festival. Talk about children who do not have enough to eat.

Music: Learn rhymes such as "Pat-a-cake, Pat-a-cake, Bakers man" or "Ten fat sausages sitting in a pan" or "Five current buns in a bakers shop" or "I'm a little tea-pot short and stout".

P.E./Movement/Drama: Practice carrying objects on a tray carefully. Act out serving people and then act the role of Mrs Wobble the Waitress.

Art & Craft: Make food from plasticine, clay, play dough etc. Collect pictures of food to make a collage. Make table decorations for your cafe. Stick pictures of food onto paper plates to serve in the cafe.

Alongside "an appropriate learning environment which provides much practical learning experience" may run a totally cross curricular theme such as:

SPRING

Language: Talk about buds/blossom growing on trees, new lambs appearing in fields, birds making nests, weather getting warmer, lighter nights and longer days, shoots appearing in the ground, people out with lawnmowers etc - all signs of spring.

Maths: Count daffodils, eggs in a nest, Easter eggs, petals on a flower etc. Make sets of different coloured flowers, large and small Easter eggs, heavy and light, tall and short spring buds.

Science & Technology: Grow bulbs and keep simple records of progress. Plant enough so that every now and then you can dig one up to see "how its getting on". Grow cress and other seeds. Talk about what we need to make seeds grow. Collect buds from trees and examine with a magnifying glass. Take a large bud apart and examine the inside. Make chicks with moving heads or legs using brass paper fasteners or make pop up Easter cards.

Humanities: Go for a walk in the school grounds/local environment. Talk about directions left, right, up and down etc. Look for change - buds on trees, shoots appearing etc. Decide what was there before - what is new - what will happen in the future. Observe the clothes people are wearing. Visit a pond and look for frogspawn.

R.E.: Talk about new life in plants. Hatch some eggs in the classroom and talk about the miracle of life.

Music: This Little Puffin - compiled by Elizabeth Matterson - Pub. by Puffin Books - a section of this book is devoted to "In the Garden".

P.E./Movement/Drama: Act out the growth of a seed from deep in the ground - stretching upwards - reaching the light - flowering - dying back etc. Make movements based on "spring" animals - chick hatching out of shell etc.

Art & Craft: Make collage of blossom on trees etc; make blossom or chicks using sponge prints; make 3D daffodils using cut-up egg cartons; colour patterns for Easter eggs. Make a farm visit and then a frieze of all the animals seen. Mark on names of young animals. Make 3D hyacinths in paper cups; toilet roll puppets of spring animals etc.

PRACTICAL TOPICS FOR THE PRIMARY SCHOOL

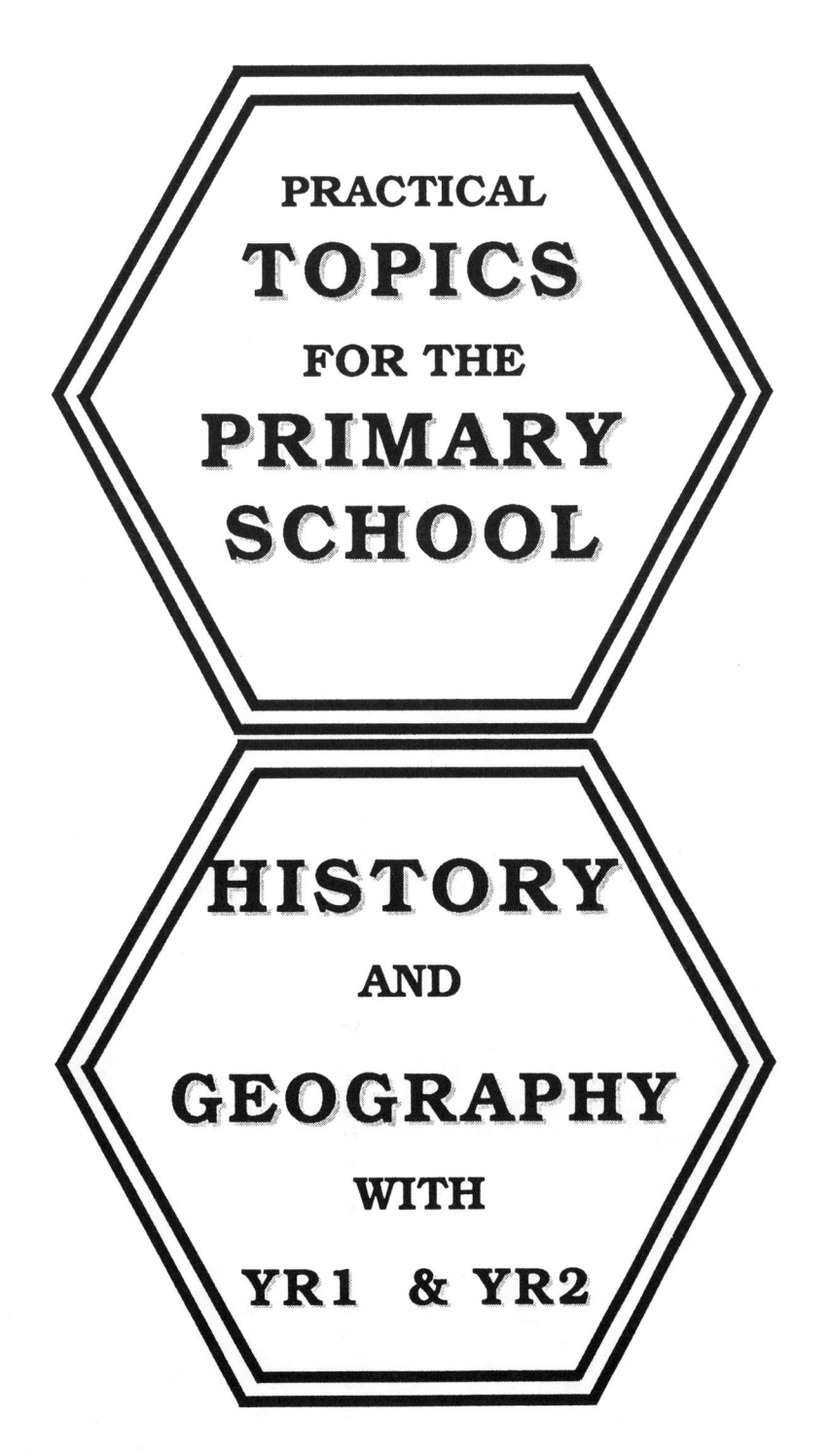

HISTORY AND GEOGRAPHY WITH YR1 & YR2

HISTORY AND GEOGRAPHY WITH YEARS 1 & 2 (Middle & Top Infants)

There are 4 aspects to this work:

(1) On-Going Activities
e.g. weather recording, listening to stories from different periods and cultures; structured play with Road mats, model farms, Model railway sets, the home corner, the shop, dressing up etc, structured play with sand and water, nature walks carried out over the same route at different times of the year. (P.T.O. for more details).

(2) The Museum Table/Far Away Table (or Interest Table)
This should be changed regularly and provide hands on experience of: old household objects, pictures and photographs, coins, newspapers etc, artifacts brought back from holiday, post-cards, photographs, simple maps and globes. Materials collected from local outings should also be displayed and experimented with. (P.T.O. for more details).

(3) Exploring Short (Vaguely Humanities) Themes
Each term would be made up of three short themes: one vaguely Science, one vaguely Humanities and one appropriate to "your" children at that point in time.

Examples of Humanities themes to be included in a two year cycle are:

Around & About Our School	My first 6 Years	A Journey to ....
When Gran and Grandad Were Young	Holidays Abroad	Life in a Castle Many Years Ago

N.B. The Topics "A Journey to ....." should be a contrast to the local area. Two examples are given in this book: "A Journey to the City .... London" and "A Journey to the Country ..... The Lake District". These examples could be adapted to include other places more familiar to pupils such as "Edinburgh" or "The Peak District" etc.

4) Information Technology (Computer Studies)

Pupils should have the opportunity to use information technology for:
(a) Simple wordprocessing.
(b) Simple graphics programs.
(c) Simple data-base programs.
(d) Simple number programs.
(e) Simple music programs.

ON-GOING WORK

Programme of Study	Activity
Children should observe and record the changes in the weather and relate these to their everyday activities. They should observe, over a period of time, the length of the day, the position of the Sun, and where possible the Moon, in the sky. They should investigate the use of a sundial as a means of observing the passage of time.	Daily weather records made by the children could be kept on an appropriate chart. In sunny weather records of the position of the sundial may also be noted. In the winter months children could be asked to look frequently for the position of the moon.
Children should observe closely their local natural environment to detect seasonal changes, including day-length, weather and changes in plants and animals, and relate these changes to the passage of time.	Children at this stage could be taken on the same local Nature Walk once each month to notice first hand the changes that take place.
Children should be taught to identify familiar landscape features such as rivers, hills, ponds, wood etc.	These features may be pointed out first hand on Nature Walks (if appropriate surroundings) or taught using pictures and photographs.
Children should listen to stories from different periods and cultures including; (a) well-known myths and legends; (b) stories about historical events; (c) eyewitness accounts of historical events; (d) fictional stories set in the past; They should be taught about the lives of different kinds of famous men and women e.g. rulers, saints, artists, engineers, explorers, inventors, pioneers etc. They should be taught about past events of different types e.g. centenaries, religious festivals, anniversaries, the Gunpowder Plot, the Olympic Games etc.	Infant story time often held at the end of a day is the ideal opportunity to read or tell stories of all kinds. Much incidental learning occurs during such occasions. Famous lives of men and women may feature in daily asemblies. Events of different types may be discussed when "in the news" or at appropriate times of the year e.g. November 5th.

INTEREST TABLE

Programme of Study	Activity
Children should collect, and find differences and similarities in, natural materials found in the locality, including rocks and soil. They should compare samples with those represented or described at second hand.	On their regular Nature walks the children may collect various items of interest, bring them back to the classroom and compare them with similar examples found in simple reference books.
Children should investigate the extent to which a selection of everyday waste products, e.g., garden refuse, paper, plastic materials and cans "decay naturally". They should keep records of their observations and use this knowledge to help improve the appearance of their local environment.	Simple experiments on decay could be set up and observed in the classroom. (Care must be taken to make sure these are safe.)
Children should identify water in different forms.	When it snows or freezes the opportunity should be taken to explore the nature of snow and ice. Activities could include feeling; observing through magnifying glasses or a binocular microscope; observing over a period of time; heating it up etc.

PROGRAMME OF STUDY

Children should name where they live, name and explore familiar features in the locality e.g. buildings, parks, places of landscape etc. They should discuss work and leisure activities and investigate use of land and buildings in the local area, including extraction of natural resources (if any). They should identify how goods and services needed in the local community are provided and look for the effects of weather on their surroundings. Investigations should be made of how and why people make journeys. Children should discuss likes and dislikes about features in the local environment, changes that have taken place and improvements which could be made.

SKILLS TO BE DEVELOPED

Research skills - see Appendix 1

Geographical skills -

Observe their surroundings and examine pictures and pictorial maps of distant places, ask questions, identify similarities and differences concerning: water, land and the weather; homes, jobs and journeys; natural and man-made environments.

Follow directions; use pictorial maps for information; draw around objects to make a plan; make plans of real/imaginary places, identify land and sea on maps and globes; follow a route on a map; use pictures and photographs to find out about places.

CURRICULUM LINKS

English	-	Compile a questionnaire about occupations and travelling to work.
Maths	-	Graph of the distance people travel to work/the types of transport used. Simple work on co-ordinates.
Science	-	Experiment with a magnet and a direction compass.
History	-	Look for evidence of changes that have taken place near your school.
R.E.	-	Visit a local church and make a plan of the inside.
P.E.	-	Practice following oral directions e.g, left, right, north, south etc.
Art	-	Use printing to create a brick texture for a model or a picture.

AROUND AND SCH

(If you have carried out this

ACTIVITIES

Learn how to make plans of simple clasroom objects.

Make plans of your table, your classroom and your school.

Make a plan of your route to school.

Make a map of your route to school using simple symbols. Compare with a real map.

Follow a set of directions to lead you to a hidden "treasure" in the school grounds.

Make a treasure island map of your own.

Look at maps and globes of the world and identify land and sea.

Follow a route on a map to see where you end up.

PLAY

Sand & water play - make a scene with a winding river, a road and a bridge.

Make a simple route for vehicles to pass through. Make a road works or quarry scene.

Role play - turn the house corner into a mini-supermarket. Include boxes of goods to fill the shelves and baskets for people to empty the shelves with.

Imaginative play - Play with road mats and toy cars; farm and animals; railway; dolls houses. All of these could be mapped!

Play with constructional toys - make buildings, barriers, tunnels etc to use with play mat and toy cars, lego airport, railways etc.

STARTING POINTS

A series of walks around planned routes close to school. These routes could include a visit to a park, the local shops, a housing estate, a factory or trading estate. Make individual maps of the route taken including as much detail as possible. Compare pupils own maps with large scale O.S. maps and aerial photographs of the area. Look for the effects of weather on older buildings.

Books

Oxford - Pre-Atlas Workbook - "Making Plans".
Picture Word Books by Usborne - The House - The Shop - The Town

RESOURCES/EQUIPMENT

Simple dictionary; slides; posters etc.
A good collection of children's books concerning houses, shops, local services etc.
A selection of large scale maps including O.S. 1:2500 and 1:10000.
A collection of pictures and photographs of a high street.

Possible Visits
A local quarry or factory.
A local farm.

Possible Visitors
A local shopkeeper to talk about how he obtains his stock.

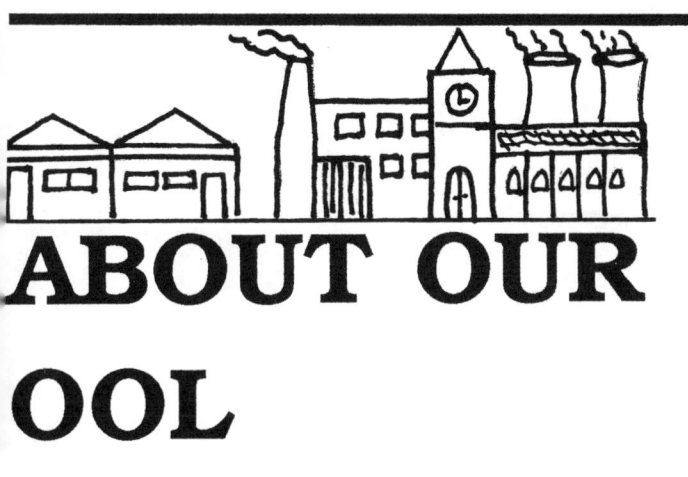

ABOUT OUR SCHOOL

Topic .... Turn to Appendix 8)

TALK ABOUT

- their address in the form of street, town and county.
- the different uses of buildings they have seen e.g. homes, shops, churches etc.
- the different uses of land seen in the area around and including the school.
- the jobs carried out by the adults around them e.g. postman, lorry driver, doctor, shopkeeper etc.
- what people do in their spare time.
- likes and dislikes in the local environment.
- improvements they would like to see.
- pictures and photographs of a high street scene.
- what a direction compass is used for.

CREATIVE WORK

Make a large group collage/picture of each of the places visited.

Make model houses and shops and create a scene with toy cars.

Make model trees for inclusion in the treasure island model.

Make a large model of a house which can be opened up to see inside.

Make a series of shop fronts in a row selling different types of goods.

Reproduce street signs found in the area.

Make rubbings of different textures in the school grounds.

END PRODUCT

Display of written and creative work or individual booklets made.

A large plan of the school in its grounds.

Large maps complete with symbols showing the "walks" undertaken by the class.

A model of a "treasure island" complete with trees, hills, sailing ship and treasure chest.

Make a display of natural items collected in the park.

Model street with houses, cars, street signs etc.

PROGRAMME OF STUDY

Children should have opportunities to investigate changes in their own lives and those of their family or adults around them.

SKILLS TO BE DEVELOPED

Research Skills - see Appendix 1

Historical skills -

Listen to stories from and ask questions about the past.

Use common words and phrases relating to the passing of time e.g. old, new, before, after, long ago, days of the week, months, years, etc.

Identify a sequence of events and talk about why they happened e.g. changes in the life of a pupil.

Observe differences between ways of life at different times in the past e.g. the clothes worn in different periods.

Distinguish between different versions of events e.g. "what happened in school last week".

Find out about the past from different types of historical source e.g. artefacts; pictures and photographs; music; adults talking about their own past; written sources; buildings and sites; computer based material.

CURRICULUM LINKS

Englsh	-	Use words such as yesterday, week, month, year, old, new, before, after, long time etc.
Maths	-	Learn the times of getting up, breakfast, lunch, tea, bedtime etc.
Science	-	Talk about life cycles. Illustrate with examples from the animal world.
Technology	-	Design a simple and safe playpen with plenty of things to keep a toddler amused.
Geography	-	Look at maps of where class members were born, now live, gone to school etc.
Music	-	Action songs to play with young children from "This Little Puffin" - Compiled by Elizabeth Matterson.
R.E.	-	Investigate how Christian families name their children and welcome them into the life of the church.
P.E.	-	Move in ways appropriate to different age groups.
Art	-	Collage picture of children of different ages playing together.

MY FI

SIX Y

(If you have carried out this

ACTIVITIES

Make simple time lines e.g. one day - order pictures of morning/afternoon/night - the order of events during one school day.

Hang different age/size clothes on washing line.

Sequence photographs of a child up to six years.

Make own personal time line. Children could describe events important to them through pictures or text.

Make a bag of "evidence" with children's artifacts. Discuss the age of the owner.

Write about yourself as a baby. Teacher reads out, class use the "evidence" to describe who each one is.

Cut up old Mothercare/Early Learning catalogues.

Arrange toys/equipment into appropriate age groups.

Interview parents in class about 'their' life e.g. Where were they born? First Memories? School? Holidays? Being a teenager? Work? etc.

PLAY

Role play - Looking after the new baby. Equip house corner with cot, pram, baby equipment etc.

Looking after a toddler. Equip house corner with fire guard, appropriate toys, large doll dressed as toddler, bibs, feeding bowls, washing machine! etc.

Imaginative Play - Recreate a Nursery School for dolls. Including activites such as painting, baking, brick play, outside play, music and dancing.

Play with constructional toys - e.g. duplo, lego, plastic meccano, brio etc. Construct cot, pram, rocking cradle, playpen etc. Use dolls to try equipment out.

STARTING POINTS

Children "interview" parents using a questionnaire about what the children were like as babies.

Make a collection of children's sweaters or shoes from age 0 - 6. Arrange in order.
Make a collection of children's toys from 0 - 6.

Talk about/collect equipment needed to look after a baby.

Create a 3D time line display - arranging items collected in appropriate order.

Ask a parent to bath a baby in school.
Discuss what a baby needs to survive.

Books

When I was a Baby - C. Anholt - Pub. Heinemann.
My Day - R. Campbell - Pub. Picture Livad.
The Red Woollen Blanket - B. Graham - Pub. Walker.
I Open My Eyes - G. Stowell - Pub. Mowbray & Co.
At School - L. Ivory - Pub. Burke Books.
Carol's Babysitter - N. Snell - Hamish Hamilton.
My Childminder - Althea - Dinosaur.

RESOURCES/EQUIPMENT

Simple dictionary; slides, posters etc.
A good collection of childrens reference and story books.

A. A. Milne poem "When I was One".
Collection of pictures showing children at different ages and stages of development.
Examples of equipment needed for looking after a baby.

Possible Visits
Visit a nursery or playgroup to see what the children are doing.
A local museum to look at 'old' things.

Possible Visitors
A mother with new baby.
A mother with "outgoing toddler" willing to talk.

RST EARS

Topic .... Turn to Appendix 8)

TALK ABOUT

- the order of events of a typical day.
- the things younger brother/sisters can/cannot do.
- things you can do now that you could not as babies.
- pictures of old and modern artifacts. Discuss which existed before themselves.
- who was alive in their family before they were.
- what their parents played with when they were little - have things changed? Video? Computer?
- pictures of old ladies, young men etc. Which person helps? Which is a burglar? Talk about bias.
- old and new.
- what you did yesterday/last week/last Christmas/last year.
- changes seen in old photographs.
- how a family prepares for a new baby.

CREATIVE WORK

Draw pictures of themselves at different stages in their life. Arrange in correct order.

Write about your very earliest memories.

Write about things your parents say you did when you were very small.

Write/paint some important memories e.g. a fantastic holiday, moving house etc.

Write/paint a picture of favourite soft toy.

Cut out pictures/make charts of food you like now and food you used to eat.

Write good and bad things about being very young.

Consider "Who cares for me?"

END PRODUCT

Display of written and creative work or individual booklets made.

Large wall time line with some very old events e.g. Dinosaurs, Romans etc showing where the children's six years fit in.

Large wall time line including photographs, toys, clothes, examples of children's work etc.

Exhibition entitled "When I Was Young". Invite parents and give a guided tour.

Make a collage of a playgroup/nursery school scene.

Christening a doll in a mock church service.

PROGRAMME OF STUDY

Children should understand that their country is part of the United Kingdom, which is made up of England, Wales, Scotland and Northern Ireland. They should investigate landscape features of a U.K. locality (different from their own) e.g. through looking at holiday postcards and photographs. They should identify and describe similarities and differences in land-use, landscape and weather between home and the area of study. They should investigate how to get there, how and why people make journeys and why different means of transport are needed. They should talk about work and leisure activities. They should understand that most homes are in settlements of varying size and how goods and services needed by the community are provided, including where natural resources are obtained from. They should discuss likes and dislikes about the environment including changes made by man.

SKILLS TO BE DEVELOPED

Research skills - see Appendix 1

Geographical skills -

Observe their surroundings and examine pictures and pictorial maps of distant places; ask questions, identify similarities and differences concerning: water, land and the weather; homes, jobs and journeys; natural and man-made environments.

Follow directions; use pictorial maps for information; draw around objects to make a plan; make plans of real/imaginary places; identify land and sea on maps and globes; follow a route on a map; use pictures and photographs to find out about places.

CURRICULUM LINKS

English	-	Make lists of adjectives to describe a noisy city street.
Maths	-	Make a graph of the different types of transport experienced by pupils.
Science	-	Talk about pollution of the air and rivers.
Technology	-	Design and build a simple model of a train.
History	-	Listen to stories of 'the Gun Powder Plot' and 'the Fire of London'.
Music	-	Listen to sounds/act out a busy city street scene/market scene.
R.E.	-	Find out about St. Paul's Cathedral.
P.E.	-	Try making precise 'changing of the guard' movements.
Art	-	Paint pictures of the flags of U.K. countries.

A Journey to ....

(If you have carried out this

ACTIVITIES

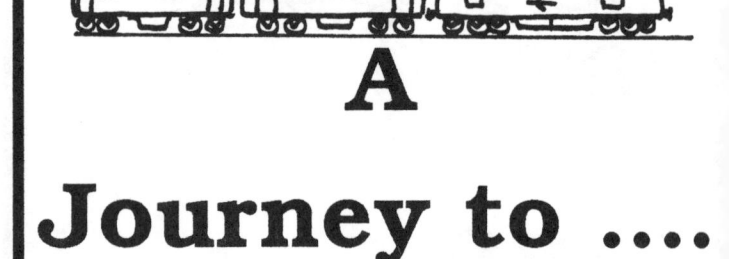

Make own maps of the United Kingdom. Colour and name the different countries.

Mark home town and London on the map.

Study holiday postcards and photographs for landscape features. Compare with home.

Talk about what the land is mainly used for in the photographs - if any landscape is visible - ask will the weather be different from home?

Look at travel brochures, time-tables, maps etc. and discuss the advantage/disadvantages of various forms of transport to London.

Interview an adult who has lived or worked in London. Talk about the distances people travel to work and why?

Talk about where food comes from and the water supply.

PLAY

Sand & Water - Make a busy port scene with lots of ships and various places for them to tie up and unload.

Role Play - Turn the home corner into a "big red bus" or "underground train". Provide rows of seats, tickets, a driver, inspector, bus stop, ticket office etc.

Imaginative Play - Use model cards, buses and trucks in a busy city environment. Include a road works scene. Use other models in a busy airport scene.

Play with constructional toys - Build tall cranes to use in the construction of wooden "tower blocks". Build various moving bridges to span a wide river that toy cars can cross and which open to let ships through.

- 58 -

STARTING POINTS

Listen to a "Bear Called Paddington" and find out how he got his name. Study a globe to see where he came from.

Plan an imaginary journey to London. Consider how to get there, where to stay and what to do.

Make a list of famous buildings/places the children have heard of/visited.

Talk about a large map at the United Kingdom which shows England, Scotland, Wales and Northern Ireland.

Books

Discovering The Tower of London - Ladybird
Discovering The National History Museum - Ladybird
Book of London - City Guide - Usbourne Books
A Bear Called Paddington - Michael Bond - Collins
Britain - Maps and Map work - Macmillan Education

RESOURCES/EQUIPMENT

Simple dictionary; slides; posters etc.

A good collection of children's books concerning the sites and activities carried out in London.

A large map of the U.K. showing physical features.
A large map of the U.K. showing towns, roads, railways and air routes. e.g. the wall maps which go with Britain - Maps and Map work by Macmillan Education.
A large road map showing motorways.
A large street/tourist map of London.
A selection of holiday postcards and photographs.
Aerial photographs.

Possible Visits
If at all possible, make a day visit to London. Visit a local railway or bus station or a local motorway service station.

Possible Visitors
Adults that have visited, lived or worked in London.

LONDON

Topic .... Turn to Appendix 8)

TALK ABOUT

- who has been to London.
- what they thought of it.
- how it was different from home.
- where it can be found on a British map.
- how we can travel there.
- where you could stay.
- the sort of things you might do during your visit.
- underground railways.
- red buses and taxis/busy noisy traffic.
- what it would be like to live in a skyscraper.
- Buckingham Palace.
- Heathrow Airport.

CREATIVE WORK

Write likes and dislikes about living in a big city.

Make individual collage/picture of one or a number of London sights.

Make own map showing the journey from your home to London. Indicate the type of transport you would use.

Make a junk model city centre scene (Each child to make a skyscraper, house, factory, etc. Fit together with lots of roads and streets). Attempt to map the finished product.

Paint pictures of postcards from a famous gallery.

Make a full size picture of a London policeman.

Make a frieze showing the changing of the guard.

END PRODUCT

Display of written and creative work or individual booklets made:

Make a large "London Skyline" on a classroom wall incorporating as many houses, cars, planes, skyscrapers, river traffic, people, famous sights as possible.

Make a mock up of a London musuem and Art Gallery. Advertise, sell tickets and have a day to give adults a conducted tour.

Make a simple London picture map showing the Thames and other famous landmarks.

Make a presentation to the rest of the school telling what has been found out.

PROGRAMME OF STUDY

Childen should understand that their country is part of the United Kingdom, which is made up of England, Wales, Scotland and Northern Ireland. They should investigate landscape features of a U.K. locality (different from their own) e.g. through looking at holiday postcards and photographs. They should identify and describe similarities and differences in land-use, landscape and weather between home and the area of study. They should investigate how to get there, how and why people make journeys and why different means of transport are needed. They should talk about work and leisure activities. They should understand that most homes are in settlements of varying size and how goods and servcices needed by the community are provided, including where natural resources are obtained from. They should discuss likes and dislikes about the environment including changes made by man.

SKILLS TO BE DEVELOPED

Research skills - see Appendix 1

Geographical skills -

Observe their surroundings and examine pictures and pictorial maps of distant places; ask questions, identify similarities and differences concerning: water, land and the weather; homes, jobs and journeys; natural and man-made environments.

Follow directions; use pictorial maps for information; draw around objects to make a plan; make plans of real/imaginary places, identify lsnd and sea on maps and globes; follow a route on a map; use pictures and photographs to find out about places.

CURRICULUM LINKS

English	-	Make a list of adjectives to describe a quiet country environment.
Maths	-	Make a graph of the different types of transport experienced by pupils.
Science	-	Talk about pollution of the air and rivers.
Technology	-	Design and build a tent for a doll to camp out in.
History	-	Draw a picture of "Muncaster Castle". - see Postman Pat Books.
Music	-	Recreate "water" sounds with various percussion instruments.
R.E.	-	Sketch pictures of "Rev. Timms" from the Postman Pat Stories. Interview a clergyman about his job.
P.E.	-	Pack an imaginary rucksack and make appropriate expedition movements.
Art	-	Make a collage of an autumn woodland.

A Journey to ....

ACTIVITIES

Make own maps of the United Kingdom. Colour and name the different countries. Mark home town and the Lake District on the map.

Study holiday postcards and photographs for landscape features. Compare with home.

Talk about what the land is mainly used for in the photographs. What is the weather like in the Lake District? Why?

Look at travel brochures, time-tables, maps etc and discuss the advantages/disadvantages of various forms of transport to the Lake District

Interview an adult who has worked or been on holiday in the Lake District. What sort of work do people there do?

Talk about where food comes from and the water supply.

PLAY

Sand and Water - Experiment with rain (watering can) coming down on sand hills. Where does the water always end up?
Does it form puddles or lakes?

Role play - turn the shop corner into a post office. Sell stamps and stationery. Have a sorting office for letters and parcels. Deliver letters with a sack to friends.

Imaginative play - Make a model hillside and use the farm to make a Lakeland Hill farm with plenty of sheep. Make model tents for dolls to go camping.

Play with constructional toys - Build a tractor and trailer to work on a farm; model farm buildings; a car and caravan for some campers.

STARTING POINTS

Listen to a number of Postman Pat stories and talk about the environment he works in.
Listen to accounts of Pat's visit to the village school. Talk about what it would be like to go to a village school.
Compare pictures in Postman Pat books with real pictures of the Lake District.
Talk about a map of the United Kingdom which shows England, Scotland, Wales and Northern Ireland.

Books

Postman Pat Books - J. Cunliffe - Hippo Books (these are based in the Lake District.)
A Lakeland Sketchbook - A. Wainwright. Pub. by Westmorland Gazette is one of many books which can be used as a source of pictures.
Britain - Maps & Mapwork - Macmillan Education.

RESOURCES/EQUIPMENT

Simple dictionary; slides; posters etc.
A good collection of books with pictures of the Lake District.
A large map of the UK showing physical features.
A large map of the UK showing towns, roads, railways and air routes e.g. the wall amps which go with Britain - Maps and Mapwork by MacMillan Education.
A large road map showing motorways.
O.S. Lake Dsitrict tourist map.
A selection of holiday postcards and photographs.
Aerial photographs.

Possible Visits
If at all possible, make a day visit to the Lake District or to the local countryside. Visit a local railway or bus station, a local motorway service station or a village school.

Possible Visitors
A climber, rambler or Lake Dsitrict enthusiast prepared to talk about their experiences.
A driver with a mobile shop. (see Postman Pat books)

THE LAKE DISTRICT

Topic .... Turn to Appendix 8)

TALK ABOUT

- who has been out in the country.
- who has been to the Lake District.
- what they thought of it.
- how it was different from home.
- where it can be found on a British map.
- how we can travel there.
- where we could stay.
- the sort of things you might do during your visit.
- what it would be like to climb a mountain.
- the sorts of boats to be found on the lakes.
- the animals that may be seen in the woods
- what it would be like to live in a tiny village.
- the services available e.g. shops, cinema etc.
- the sort of work you may do.

CREATIVE WORK

Write likes and dislikes about living in the countryside.

Make individual collage/pictures of farm animals.

Make own map showing the journey from your home to the Lake District. Indicate the type of transport you would use.

Paint pictures from postcards of Lake District scenes.

Make a full size picture of Postman Pat.

Listen to a Postman Pat story and make a map of a journey he made.

END PRODUCT

Display of written and creative work or individual booklets made.

Make a large "Lakeland Skyline" on a classroom wall incorporating fells, lakes, villages, climbers, farms, traffic etc.

Make a class model with mountains, streams running down, a farm, a lake at the lowest point, roads, stone walls etc.

Make individual picture maps of the model.

Make a frieze of Postman Pat at work.
Include as many of his friends as possible.

PROGRAMME OF STUDY

Children should have opportunities to investigate changes in the way of life of British people since the Second World War.

Progressing from familiar situations to those more distant in time and place, pupils should be taught about the everyday life, work, leisure and culture of men, women and children in the past e.g. clothes, houses, diet, shops, jobs, transport, entertainment, etc.

SKILLS TO BE DEVELOPED

Research Skills - see Appendix 1

Historical Skills -

Listen to stories from and ask questions about the past.

Use common words and phrases relating to the passing of time e.g. old, new, before, after, long ago, days of the week, months, years, etc.

Identify a sequence of events and talk about why they happened e.g. changes in the life of a pupil.

Observe differences between ways of life at different times in the past e.g. the clothes worn in different periods.

Distinguish between different versions of events e.g. "what happened in school last week".

Find out about the past from different types of historical source e.g. artefacts; pictures and photographs; music; adults talking about their own past; written sources; buildings and sites; computer based material.

CURRICULUM LINKS

English	-	Write articles for a fifties newspaper and print using computer and appropriate program.
Maths	-	Make block graphs which show how old our grans/grandads are.
Science	-	Talk about body changes from babies to grandparents. Test the best materials to keep you warm and dry.
Technology	-	Design an ideal home for an older person.
Geography	-	Examine recent and fifties large scale maps of your area for change.
Music	-	Listen to music of the period and comment.
R.E.	-	Sensitively explore the reason for some children not having a grandparent.
P.E.	-	Rock and Roll and Hula Hoop.
Art	-	Make life size collage picture showing clothes, hairstyles of time etc.

WHEN GRAN WERE

(If you have carried out this

ACTIVITIES

Make simple Time lines from: family photographs; photographs of one person at different ages; pictures of cars, aeroplanes etc.

Place in time order old radios, cameras, newspapers or other household items.

Place in time order a very old event mixed with more familiar modern events.

Research from collections of simple information subjects such as clothes, holidays, school, transport, The Coronation, Everest etc.

Examine an old School Log Book for events which happened in school during the 50's.

Talk about a woman's role then and now.

Discuss how families provide for their oldest members.

PLAY

Role Play - Turn the house/shop corner into a house/shop of the 50's. Use appropriate artifacts - leave out television etc. Equip with appropriate dressing up clothes.

Imaginative play - Provide Andy Pandy/Wooden Top/Bill and Ben string puppets. Let children make up own stories and show rest of class.

Play with model toy cars of the 50's.

Play with constructional toys - Attempt to make models using original steel meccanno.

Design the interior of a bungalow with bricks etc Use dolls to show where everything is.

STARTING POINTS

Invite gran and grandad to afternoon tea in the classroom and chat generally with them.

Invite one or two grans/grandads to be formally interviewed from a prepared list of questions.

Make a collection of old photographs, postcards, newspapers, household objects etc from the 50's.

Hold a "Fifties Day" in school.

Devise a questionnaire and send it home for grandparents to fill in.

Books
Grannies and Grandads - Perry & Wildman - A. & C. Black.
My Grandma Has Black Hair - Hoffman & Burroughs Methuen.
When I Was Little - M. Williams - Walker Books.
The Bedspread - S. Fair - Picture Mac.
Even Granny Was Young Onec - E. Janikovsky Dobson.
Katie Morag and the Two Grandmothers - Picture Lions.
Mary and Her Grandmother - Egger & Jucker - Viking Kestrel

RESOURCES/EQUIPMENT

Simple dictionary; slides; posters etc.
A good collection of children's reference books on recent history and long ago.
B.B.C T.V Video - Watch With Mother.
Old Picture Post magazines.
B.B.C TV Watch programme of the 50's.
Boxes of artifacts/clothing from museum service.
Pathe News Videos of 1953.
Collection of 50's newspaper advertisements.
Cassette of 50's popular music.

Possible Visits
Visit a local newspaper office and examine newspapers from the fifties.
Examine local buildings in the area for evidence of their age. Sketch some fifties buildings.

Possible Visitors
Grans and Grandads. A local historian. Museum education officer.

GRAN & DAD YOUNG

Topic .... Turn to Appendix 8)

TALK ABOUT

- how we heat our homes.
- the machines we have in the home to help us.
- the type of foods we eat each week.
- the things people do in their spare time.
- how people travel from place to place.
- the sort of shops we visit.
- the names given to the money we use.
- our favourite games.
- the places we visit for holidays.

Compare all of these with life in the 50's.

- how far back we can remember.
- famous people who lived years ago.
- who do you think was alive in your family 40 years ago?
- changes in your local building including how and why they occurred.
- the answers given by grandparents to your questions.

CREATIVE WORK

Make up your own advertisement for a product of the 50's.

Make a large frieze of a typical living room showing furniture, fire, household appliances, a family at play etc.

Write a poem about your grandparents.

Make a card to give to a grandparent.

Make sweets/cook a cake as a present for a grandparent.

Make a list of words which explore feelings towards people we love.

Write about the good and bad things of being old.

END PRODUCT

Make up individual booklets of children's work.

Display written and creative work.

Put on a "Fifties" exhibition. Ask parents, Grandparents, friends etc to visit. Give guided tours around the exhibition.

Make a display of children's toys from the 50's.

Hold a competition to see who can identify Grandparents from photographs of when they were young.

Make a presentation to the rest of the school describing information of interest discovered.

PROGRAMME OF STUDY

Children should be able to name the country in which they live. They should investigate landscape features of an "overseas" locality e.g. through looking at holiday postcards, photographs, books or travel brochures. They should identify and describe similarities and differences in land-use, landscape and weather between home and the area of study. They should investigate how to get there, how and why people make journeys and why different means of transport are needed. They should talk about work and leisure activities. They should understand that most homes are in settlements of varying size and how goods and services needed by the community are provided, including where natural resources are obtained from. They should discuss likes and dislikes about the environment including changes made by man.

SKILLS TO BE DEVELOPED

Research skills - see Appendix 1

Geographical skills

Observe their surroundings; and examine pictures and pictorial maps of distant places; ask questions, identify similarities and differences concerning: water, land and the weather; homes, jobs and journeys; natural and man-made environments.

Follow directions; use pictorial maps for information; draw around objects to make a plan; make plans of real/imaginary places, identify land and sea on maps and globes; follow a route on a map; use pictures and photographs to find out about places.

CURRICULUM LINKS

English	-	Write a postcard home from your holiday abroad.
Maths	-	Graph of popular holiday destinations.
Science	-	Make simple paper planes. Which flies furthest?
Technology	-	Design and build a model ferry to carry toy cars.
History	-	Find out about the history of the hovercraft or aeroplane.
Music	-	Listen to music from different countries and comment.
R.E.	-	Draw a place of worship from a foreign country.
Art	-	Make a travel mural showing many different kinds of transport.

HOLIDAYS

(If you have carried out this

ACTIVITIES

Colour in sea and land on a simple map of Europe. Mark the United Kingdom.

List similarities and differences identified in selected foreign pictures.

Compare weather with home country.

Ask the question "Are all foreign towns holiday places?" Also, what sort of work is carried out and what do locals do in their spare time?

Make a survey of types of place visited e.g. tiny village, town, big city etc.

Consider where drinking water comes from e.g. the French drink mainly bottled water.

Follow a route on a map to Italy. Which countries need to be crossed?

PLAY

Sand and Water - Make a sea-side scene using dolls, deck-chairs, tables etc.

Role play - Convert the shop into a Travel Agents. Use out of date brochures, toy money, tickets etc. Interview children about where they want to go and type into pretend or real computer.

Imaginative play - set up a pretend harbour to handle cars and ferries. Have one on each side of a pretend sea.

Play with constructional toys - Look at pictures of docks and airports. Construct cranes, ships, planes and aircraft hangers.

STARTING POINTS

Make a class collection of postcards from abroad, dolls, foreign artifacts etc. Discuss if these are typical of everyday life.

Talk about how we can get to a foreign country, why people make such journeys and the types of transport used.

Talk about typical food eaten in other countries. Have a food tasting session.

Books

First Book of France - Usborne.
Forst Book of America - Usborne.
Beginners Language Topics - French Phrases; German Phrases; Spanish Phrases - Usborne.
Out of date travel brochures from your local travel agent.

RESOURCES/EQUIPMENT

Simple dictionary, slides, posters etc.
A good collection of children's reference books telling of everyday life in other countries.
A large world political map.
A simple globe.
A large map of the U.K. showing ports and airports.
A simple picture atlas.
A collection of postcards and photographs.
B.B.C Watch - series on France.

Possible Visits
A local port, airport or travel agent.
A short ride on a train.

Possible Visitors
A Travel Agent. A visitor from another country.

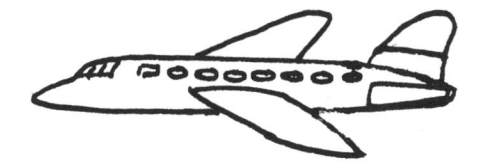

ABROAD

Topic .... Turn to Appendix 8)

TALK ABOUT

- where the children have been on holiday.
- where "abroad" is!
- what they thought of it.
- how it was different from home.
- where it can be found in an atlas or on a globe.
- how we can travel there.
- where we could stay.
- the sort of things you might do during your visit.
- what the weather was like.
- the sort of jobs they observed people doing.
- the services available e.g. shops, cinema etc.
- the different types of landscape features seen in holiday pictures and postcards.

CREATIVE WORK

Write likes and dislikes about visiting a place shown in a picture.

Make imitation passports. Include a drawing and description of yourself.

Make a list of the things you need for a holiday in ....

Make model ships, planes and hovercraft.

Draw a route from your house to Spain showing the different types of transport you would use.

Make collage pictures of traditional dress.

Paint flags from different countries.

END PRODUCT

Display of written and creative work or individual booklets made.

Take the class on an imaginary journey. Pack suitcases, stamp passports, fly in a plane, ride a coach, unpack at hotel, relax on beach etc.

Make a model airport scene with buildings, runways, planes etc.

Make a model dockyard scene with car ferry, ramp, lighthouse etc.

Learn some common English phrases in another language.

PROGRAMME OF STUDY

Children should have opportunities to investigate the way of life of people in a period of the past beyond living memory.

Progressing from familiar situations to those more distant in time and place, pupils should be taught about the everyday life, work, leisure and culture of men, women and children in the past e.g. clothes, houses, diet, shops, jobs, transport, entertainment.

SKILLS TO BE DEVELOPED

Research skills - see Appendix 1

Historical Skills -

Listen to stories from and ask questions about the past.

Use common words and phrases relating to the passing of time e.g. old, new, before, after, long ago, days of the week, months, years, etc.

Identify a sequence of events and talk about why they happened e.g. changes in the life of a pupil.

Observe differences between ways of life at different times in the past e.g. the clothes worn in different periods.

Distinguish between different versions of events e.g. "what happened in school last week".

Find out about the past from different types of historical source e.g. artefacts; pictures and photographs; music; adults talking about their own past; written sources; buildings and sites; computer based material.

CURRICULUM LINKS

English	-	Write a simple description of a castle.
Science	-	Construct simple catapult using elastic bands and test performance.
Technology	-	Look at pictures and then invent your own machine for attacking a castle.
Geography	-	Draw a plan of a castle. Label the rooms.
R.E.	-	Find out about the way of life of a monk.
Music	-	Listen to examples of medieval music. Learn to play on the recorder.
P.E.	-	Act out a castle under attack.
Art	-	Make a huge castle collage to fill one wall of the classroom.

LIFE IN A CASTLE

(If you have carried out this

ACTIVITIES

Make simple time lines which show some of the events between now and then.

Make up a story of a Knight's adventures.

Learn some names for different parts of a castle.

Talk about Heraldry and design a coat of arms for your own family.

Dress a child in parts of a reproduction suit of armour. Talk about what it feels like to wear this. Make detailed sketches.

Talk about how pople dressed - colour appropriate pictures of ordinary people.

Make a collection of castle pictures from magazines and newspapers.

PLAY

Sand and Water play - Make a simple model castle with real water in the moat. Plan an attack with appropriate figures.

Role play - Turn the home corner into a "mini" banqueting hall and hold a feast with your friends.

Imaginative play - Play with a toy castle and a selection of model figures.

Play with constructional toys - Build castles of various shapes and sizes using a selection of constructional toys.

STARTING POINTS

Make a class visit to a local castle.

Make a collection of the children's books with pictures of castles inside.

Make a full size picture/3D model of a knight in a suit of armour.

Read and talk about "The Black Knight's Plot" and/or "Queen of the Tournament" by N. & T Morns - pub. by Hodder & Stoughton.

Books

Norman Castles - Stanier & Sutton - B.B.C. Publications.
Knights & Castles - Time Traveller series - Usborne.
Castle Life - Althea - Dinosaur Publications.
Knights & Castles - Kingfisher Explorer Books.
Heraldry - J. Brooke - Little - Blackwell.

RESOURCES/EQUIPMENT

Simple dictionary; slides; posters etc.
A good collection of childrens reference and story books.
Usborne Cut Out models - Make this Model Castle - also available; model village; model town; model cathedral.
B.B.C. Zig Zag - Norman Castles.
Borrow reproduction armour from a schools museum service.

Possible Visits
A medieval castle or abbey.
Local museum to look for artifacts of long ago.

Possible Visitors
Museum education officer.
A modern day monk.

.....many years ago

Topic .... Turn to Appendix 8)

TALK ABOUT

- why were castles built?
- what were they built of?
- who lived in them?
- the sort of work they did.
- what they ate.
- how they dressed.
- how they entertained themselves.
- how comfortable it would be to live in a castle.
- who would be alive during these times.
- living in a castle under siege.
- the types of transport available.
- the sorts of furniture they used.

CREATIVE WORK

Sketch and draw plans of a castle visited by the class.

Make full size model shields and paint with own coat of arms.

Make full size swords and helmets.

Make individual/small group/whole class model of a castle. Include as many features as possible.

Make a collage of a castle kitchen showing preparations being made for a feast.

Paint pictures of life in a castle.

END PRODUCT

Display of written and creative work or individual booklets made.

A giant cross-section of a castle showing activity in each of the various rooms.

Dress up in simple costume.

Hold a banquet with appropriate entertainment.

Make a large model castle suitable for some of the "dolls" to play in.

Make a large frieze of a jousting competition.

Carry out a mock battle for possession of a castle on the school field.

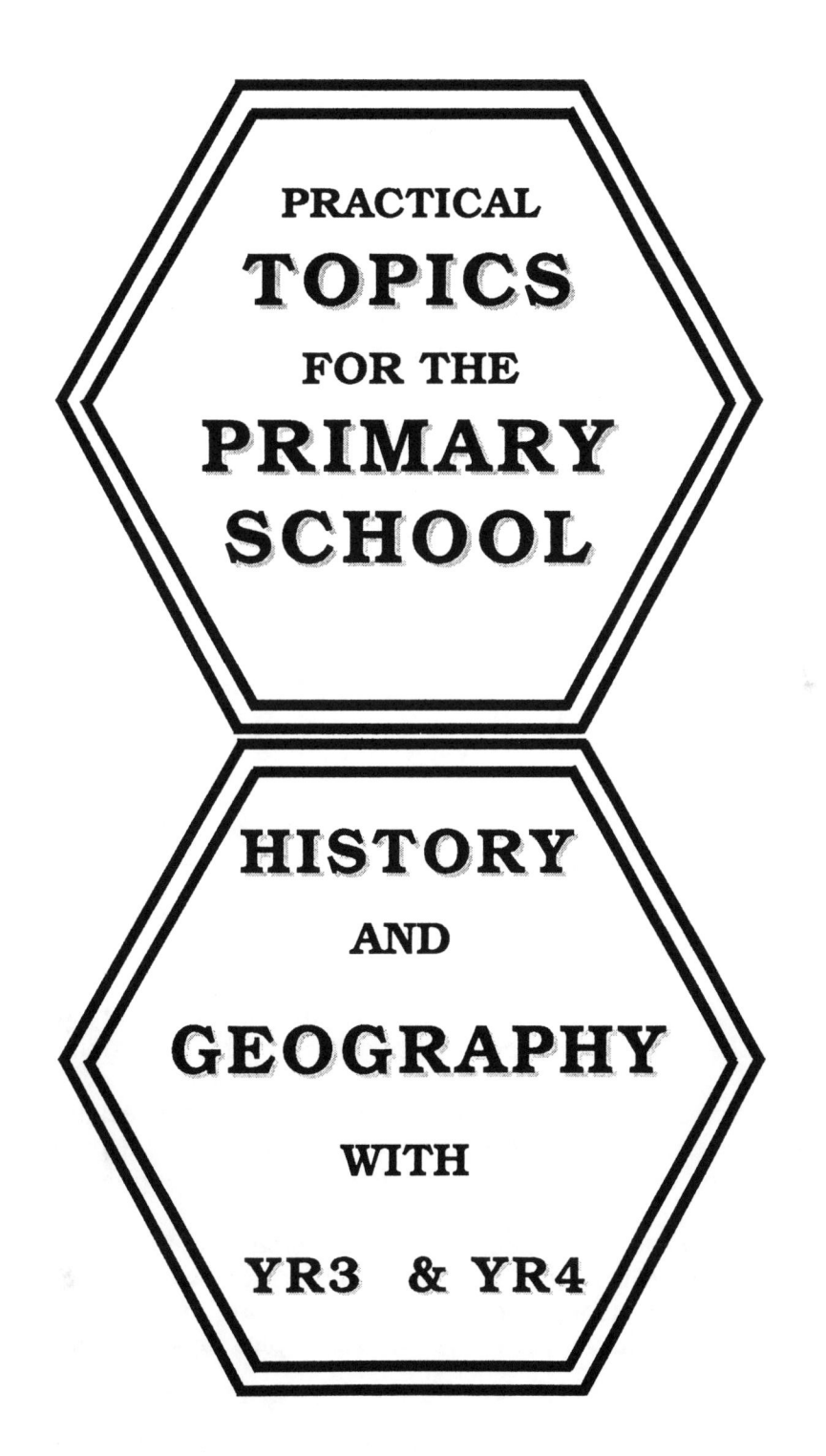

PRACTICAL TOPICS FOR THE PRIMARY SCHOOL

HISTORY AND GEOGRAPHY WITH YR3 & YR4

HISTORY & GEOGRAPHY WITH YEARS 3 & 4 (Lower Juniors)

At this level the topics should have a recognisable bias towards either History or Geography. The themes will last approximately half a term and should include research and practical activities. Six themes in a two year cycle require three major Humanities topics to be carried out each academic year. Science and Technolocgy topics will be carried out during the remaining half terms.

Humanities Topics - Years 3 & 4 - Two Year Cycle

History	Geography	R.E.
Ancient Civilisations - Egypt & Greece	Village, Town or City? - a local study.	
Invaders and Settlers	The U.K. and its Regions	Writing & Printing "Special Books"

Weighting Within a Topic

The History Topic "Ancient Civilisations" is made up of 50% History Core Study Unit 5 - Ancient Greece and 50% History Supplementary Study Unit - Section C - Ancient Egypt.

The History Topic "Invaders and Settlers" focuses on Roman, Anglo-Saxon and Viking invasions and settlements. Pupils should have opportunities to learn how British society was shaped by invading peoples and then study in greater depth one of the three invasions.

The R.E. Topic Writing & Printing "Special Books" is made up of 50% History Supplementary Study Unit - Section A - Writing and Printing, and 50% R.E. work on "Special Books". The Topic will include study of writing and printing over a long period of time. Details for the development of this topic will be found in Practical Topics for ther Primary School - Part 3 - available later.

"the effect of different surfaces and slopes on rainwater when it reaches the ground" and "to identify water in different forms" - from the Geography programme of study - should be included in the Experimental Science Topic "Water and Growth".

"learn about activities intended to improve the local environment" - from the Geography programme of study - should be included in the Natural Science Topic "In and Around a Wood/Park/Wasteland".

Art and Craft

As well as the many creative activities possible within the topics, specific Art and Craft lessons may be used to teach techniques such as fine drawing, use of colour, clay work, tie and dye, marbling, printing, use of different media such as pastels, chalks, charcoal, needlework and textiles etc. An excellent resource for the non-specialist Art teacher which follows a scheme is "Teaching Art in Primary Schools" by Geoff Rowswell published by Collins Educational.

Information Technology (Computer Studies)

Pupils should have the opportunity to use information technology for:

(a) Word processing.
(b) Data-base work.
(c) Graphics.
(d) Turtle graphics.
(e) Musical Composition.
(f) Adventure programs.

PROGRAMME OF STUDY

Pupils should be introduced to the civilisation of ancient Greece and its legacy to the modern world. The focus should be on the way of life, beliefs and achievements of the ancient Greeks.

Pupils should be taught about:

The City State
Athens and Sparta; citizens and slaves.
The Economy
Agriculture and trade; sea transport.
Everyday Life
The lives of men, women and children,; sport.
Greek religion and thought
Greek gods and religious practice; myths and legends; scientists and philosophers.
The Arts
Architecture, art, drama and literature, and how they reflected Greek society;.
Relations with other peoples
The Persian Wars; Greece and Rome.
The Legacy of Greece
Language, politics, sport and the arts
plus similar work on Ancient Egypt.

SKILLS TO BE DEVELOPED

Research skills - see Appendix I
Historical Skills

Use words and phrases relating to the passage of time including ancient, medieval, modern, B.C., A.D., Century etc.

Develop a sense of chronology by sequencing periods in history and events within those periods.

Make connections between different periods of history and different features of past societies.

Be aware of the legacies left behind from a period in history e.g. Florence Nightingale's work improved hospital conditions. Roman constructed roads improved communications.

Investigate differences between versions of past events and examine reasons why they differ e.g. World War II memories.

Extract information from and comment on a range of historical sources related to a task e.g. World War II documents, artifacts, pictures, photographs, music etc.

CURRICULUM LINKS

English	-	Make a model Greek theatre. Act out a simple play with figures.
Maths	-	Answer 4 rules of number questions using an Abacus. Construct model pyramids from nets.
Science	-	Design and test a simple means of moving heavy blocks of rock e.g a brick.
Technology	-	Design an underground tomb using traditional materials to deter robbers.
Geography	-	Find out what a quarry is and what materials are extracted.
R.E.	-	Research the names of Greek Gods, their roles and sketch carefully. Research everyday life in an Egyptian Temple.
P.E.	-	Recreate some early Olympic events.
Art	-	Make a large collage picture of Tutankhamun's death mask or Greek Gods.

Ancient Civ
EGYPT &

(If you have carried out this

WHOLE CLASS ACTIVITIES

Discuss what an "Ancient Civilisation" is and the sort of life that went on before them.

Introduce terms, A.C. and B.C.

Make a time line showing where Ancient Civilisatins fit into the order of things.

Make a time line showing some important events in the times of Ancient Greece.

Listen to stories of Athens, Sparta and the Persian Wars. Talk about Greek Science, inventions, medicine, astronomy, mathematics etc.

Make a time line showing some important events in the times of Ancient Egypt.

Talk about the nineteenth century excavations of Egyptian graves; how Egyptian society was structured; preservation of bodies and the next life etc.

SMALL GROUP ACTIVITIES

Memorise a Greek story to tell someone at home (tradition of story telling before printing).

Create a full size picture of a Greek soldier.

Make maps showing where Greece and Egypt are.

Make large scale maps of Greece and Egypt.

Make a frightening collage of a Greek monster for Odysseus to overcome.

Research and write messages in Egyptian hieroglyphics. Make a wall frieze with hieroglyphics. around the edges.

Try carving simple statues from soap.

STARTING POINTS

Listen to the story of "The Wooden Horse" and the Siege of Troy.

Dramatize the story of Pandora's box.

Estimate using time lines just where Ancient Civilisations fit !

Discuss how we know about these ancient events.

Recommended Reference Books

Looking at Ancient History - R. J. Unstead - Pub. A. & C. Black.
Everyday Life - Ancient Egypt - Usborne books.
Everyday Life - Ancient Greece - Usborne books.
The Greeks - Stainer and Sutton - B.B.C. Publications.
Egypt - S. & P. Harrison - B.B.C. Fact Finders.
The World of Odysseus - B.B.C. fact Finders.
The Ancient Greeks Activity Book - British Museum Pub.
The Ancient Egyptians Activity Book - British Museum Pub.

RESOURCES/EQUIPMENT

Dictionary, Encyclopaedia, slides, posters etc.
A good collection of simple children's reference books on Ancient Egypt & Ancient Greece.
Dig Out - Computer simulation of an archaeological dig
A.V.P. software.
B.B.C. Zig Zag - The Ancient Greeks.
B.B.C. T.V. - Odyssey.
B.B.C. Landmarks - Egypt.
Usborne Cut-Out models - Make this Egyptian Temple.

Possible Visits
Local museum to examine typical items unearthed by an archaeological dig.

Possible Visitors
Museum curator/education officer.
Amateur archaeologist.

Best Time of Year
Any.

ilisations GREECE

Topic .... Turn to Appendix 8)

CREATIVE WORK

Listen to written accounts; examine pictures; discuss and then write:

The Diary of a person opening Tutankhamun's tomb for the first time in hundreds of years.

An adventure based on a long and difficult journey (an Odyssey).

Recreate patterns from Egyptian dress or Greek vases.

Talking and Listening

Listen to some Greek Myths e.g. Jason and the Golden Fleece.
Talk about the poet Homer, the Iliad and the Odyssey.
Debate the role of slaves.
Talk about the difference between 'a story' and 'history' and how we know so much about Ancient Greece.
Listen to some Egyptian Myths and legends. Dsicuss why the people thought in these ways. Listen to the story of Cleopatra.
Talk about how we know so much about Ancient Egypt.

INDIVIDUAL ACTIVITIES

Make up individual topic booklets containing stories written and information collected.

Research Greek farming, trade, dress, food, sport, education, pottery etc.

Build model Greek buildings.

Make a model of the Trojan Horse.

Make a model Greek galleon; chariots etc.

Make model vases from clay.

Research Egyptian farming, crafts, banquets, games, houses, food, music etc.

Make a model Egyptian funeral boat; copies of Egyptian jewelry; simple house, obelisk etc.

END PRODUCT

Display of written and creative work in individual booklets made.

Make a large frieze/collage of an Ancient Greek market place or use models to recreate a market place scene.

Use models to recreate an archaeological dig in the Valley of the Kings.

Create a scene inside an Egyptian Tomb just rediscovered by archaeologists. Recreate as many artifacts as possible e.g. Throne, Mask, Weapons, Sandals, wall paintings etc.

PROGRAMME OF STUDY

This work should be carried out with Map A from N.C. Geog. guidelines as well as large scale local and pupil made maps.

Children should be able to mark on a map of the British Isles approximately where they live. They should classify landscape features and industrial and leisure activities which they have observed in the local area; offer reasons for the location of specified activities; observe and explain the relationships between land-use, buildings and human activities; explain where economic activities are located.

Children should be able to identify and describe landscape features including river, hill, valley, lake and beach. They should investigate how the functions and origins of settlements are revealed by their features. They should study how land is used in different ways and why different amounts of land are required for different purposes.

SKILLS TO BE DEVELOPED
Research Skills - See Appendix 1

Geographical Skills -

Use pictures to identify features/find out about places and then describe using geographical terms.

Interpret symbols, measure direction and distance, follow routes and describe the location of places using maps.

Make representations of real or imaginary places; make and use maps of routes, and sketch maps of small areas showing the main features and using symbols with keys.

Use the eight points of the compass.

Determine the straight line distance between two points on a map.

Use letter and number co-ordinates and four-figure grid references to locate features on a map.

Locate their position and identify features outside the classroom using a large-scale map.

Identify features on vertical aerial photographs and match them to a map.

Use maps to find out where features are located and where activities take place.

Find information in an atlas using the index and contents pages.

CURRICULUM LINKS

English	-	Compose a letter to the council with suggestions for improving your area.
Maths	-	Make graphs which show the types of houses pupils live in.
Science	-	Research how electricity is made.
Technology	-	Design and build a working model showing a power station supplying electricity for street lights.
History	-	Use local history books to find out how your community originated.
Music	-	Research what facilities are available to hear live music?
R.E.	-	Research what facilities are available for different religious groups.
P.E.	-	Dramatize the different roles played by people in a busy community.
Art	-	Experiment with various media to represent the materials used in local buildings.

VILLAGE, TO

(A local

(If you have carried out this

WHOLE CLASS ACTIVITIES

Draw/colour individual maps of Great Britain marking important towns/features and your village/town/city.

Study large scale copies of local maps.

Learn approximate scales and some symbols.

Devise an appropriate means of gathering information on local land use and carry it out.

Make a very large pupil made map showing as much of the local area as possible.

Learn the names of some natural landscape features. Get out and visit local examples or study pictures and photographs.
Find out how these features are marked on O.S. maps.

Discuss the reasons for "your" settlement being where it is and look for evidence to confirm your beliefs.

SMALL GROUP ACTIVITIES

Make your own large scale map of part of your area showing different land uses.

Devise your own symbols to show land use.

Use written instructions to follow routes on large scale maps.

Compare maps of different scale but of the same area.

Make a plan which shows the different uses of space in your school e.g. learning, moving, storage etc.

Use a Silva compass to follow a set route around your school grounds.

Match aerial photographs to their positions on a map.

Build models of houses, shops, churches etc. to be used in the class model town.

STARTING POINTS

Discuss and research the definitions of hamlet, village, town, suburb, city, etc.

Debate which category your community comes into.

Study maps of Great Britain (or make large wall map) and note where your community is placed).

Make a survey (or go out and examine) the land use in your community. e.g. housing, shopping, farming, industry, leisure etc.

Use large scale maps to study further the different land uses in your area.

Recommended Reference Books

Charlie and Chocolate Factory (Industrial awareness)
R. Dahl - Puffin
The Town   - Watson & King - Usbourne Books.
How a Town Works - Howard - Macdonald Educational
Britain - Maps & Mapwork - Macmillan Education

RESOURCES/EQUIPMENT

Dictionary, Encyclopeadia, slides, posters etc.
A good collection of simple children's reference books concerning towns, shops, services etc.
A class set of atlases which can be used to locate your village, town or city.
A selection of large scale maps of the area e.g. local street maps; O.S. 1" series, 1:2500, 1:10000 etc.   A selection of local postcards, directories, local history books, aerial photographs etc.

Possible Visits

Local council chambers; local trading estate; housing estate; shopping centre; leisure centre etc.
A local high point to "look down on your community".
A local industry to see how a raw material is turned into a useful product.

Possible Visitors

Town planner; the Mayor; businessman; fireman; health visitor etc. to talk about "their patch".

Best Time of Year

Spring - Summer - Autumn.

WN OR CITY?
study)

Topic .... Turn to Appendix 8)

CREATIVE WORK

Listen to written accounts; examine pictures; discuss and then write.

Sleeping out in a cardboard box.
Loneliness.
The things I do in my spare time.
What I would like to do in my spare time if only ......

Talking and Listening

Talk about the different uses made of land in your area, why you think these have come about and how much land each activity takes.
Talk about where supermarkets get their food, dairies their milk, taps their water, postmen their letters etc.
Interview an older member of your community to find out how things have changed.
Talk about the role of the Mayor and local government.

INDIVIDUAL ACTIVITIES

Make up individual topic booklet containing stories written and information collected.

Research the supplies to the shops, how certain manufactured goods are made, the work of the police/fire/hospital services etc.

Make pictures of local land use.

Make pictures of an environment different from yours.

Make a map with symbols and a key of your route to school.

Use four figure grid references to locate features on a local map.

Calculate the distance between two features on a map.

END PRODUCT

Display of written and creative work or individual booklets made:

A large wall pupil made map showing use of land in the area.

A class model of a fictious (or partially factual) town/city which includes roads, airport, docks, railway, various types of housing, shopping areas, churches, industry and services e.g. police, fire, hospital, garages, cinema etc.

A collage/mural showing examples of local land use in action amidst appropriate natural features.

PROGRAMME OF STUDY

Pupils should be introduced to the early history of the Biritsh Isles. They should have opportunities to learn how British society was shaped by invading peoples. The focus should be on Roman, Anglo-Saxon and Viking invasions and settlements and on Britain as part of a wider European world. Pupils should be taught about:

Invasions and settlements from 55 BC to the early eleventh century: The Roman conquest and settlement of Britain; resistance to Roman rule, including Boudicca; Britain as part of the Roman Empire; the departure of the Legions.
Anglo-Saxon invasions and settlements, including the rule of Alfred, King of Wessex; the conversion of England by Roman and Celtic Christians.
Viking raids and settlement; Britain as part of a wider Viking world.

Pupils should have opportunitires to study in greater depth one of the three invasions, the motives which prompted it, the way of life of settlers and of the peoples whom they conquered. They should be taught about
Reasons for invasion: The search for land, trade and raw materials.
Way of life of the settlers: Everyday life in town and country; houses and home life; religious life.
The legacy of settlement: Place names and language; myths and legends; styles of art and architecture.

SKILLS TO BE DEVELOPED

Research skills - see Appendix I

Historical Skills -

Use words and phrases relating to the passage of time including ancient, medieval, modern, B.C., A.D., Century etc.

Develop a sense of chronology by sequencing periods in history and events within those periods.

Make connections between different periods of history and different features of past societies.

Be aware of the legacies left behind from a period in history e.g. Florence Nightingale's work improved hospital conditions. Roman constructed roads improved communications.

Investigate differences between versions of past events and examine reasons why they differ e.g. World War II memories.

Extract information from and comment on a range of historical sources related to a task e.g. World War II documents, artifacts, pictures, photographs, music etc.

CURRICULUM LINKS

English	-	Investigate how the Romans gave us the name of our months.
Maths	-	Work with Roman numbers.
Science	-	Experiment with various items buried during the length of the topic - which items do/do not change?
Technology	-	Design and construct a working model of a Roman aquaduct.
Geography	-	Use maps to study the extent of the Roman Empire and the routes taken by Roman roads in Britain.
R.E.	-	Investigate Roman Gods and how Christianity was brought to Britain.
P.E.	-	Practice marching with Roman swords and shields. Devise defensive positions..
Art	-	Investigate various ways of making coloured squares and create mosaic designs.

Invaders &

Settlers ...

(If you have carried out this

WHOLE CLASS ACTIVITIES

Discuss and write briefly about early British History i.e. Stone Age; Bronze Age; Iron Age; Ancient Britons etc.

Talk about why the Romans came; how they conquered and the fact that they created settlements.

Talk about life as part of the Roman empire and why the legions finally departed.

Make a time line through history showing when the Romans invaded Britain.

Make Roman shields and swords and practice military manoeuvres in the school hall.

Dress a child in Roman costume or armour for others to sketch.

Make life size model/collage of Roman soldier.

SMALL GROUP ACTIVITIES

Research facts about Hadrian's Wall. Build a model including a simple mile castle.

Make a scale drawing of a Roman Fort.

Construct a plan of a typical Roman town.

Describe in detail a visit to a Roman bath house.

Draw a detailed plan or make a simple model of a Roman central heating system.

Sketch and label the main parts of a typical Roman villa.

Examine artifacts from a museum loan - debate uses and make careful sketches.

Construct a map of the Roman Empire.

Draw and colour chariots for a race frieze.

STARTING POINTS

Listen to a class novel set in Roman times e.g. 'The Eagle of the Ninth by Rosemary Sutcliff' or 'Word of Caesar by Geoffrey Treace'.

Visit to local Roman remains or Roman road.

Visit to local museum to look for evidence of Roman presence in the area.

Construction of a model Roman road or of a section of Hadrian's Wall.

Construction of full size Roman Soldier dressed in appropriate armour.

Discussion of various nations that have invaded this country.

Recommended Reference Books

From Cavemen to Vikings - R. J. Unstead - Published by A & C Black.
Living in Roman Times - Usborne First History
Ancient Rome - Usborne Everday Life
Romans activity book - British Museum
The Romans - Tim Wood - Paperbird (Ladybird)

RESOURCES/EQUIPMENT

Dictionary, Encyclopaedia, slides, posters etc.
A good collection of children's reference books on Roman Times.
Usborne cut-out-models - "Make this Roman Fort" - possibly assembled by a parent.
Local museum loan of artifacts or replicas.
B.B.C - Watch - TV Series "The Romans".
Archaeology - open-ended computer program about an archaeological dig - Cambridgeshire Software House.

Possible Visits
Local Roman remains such as Hadrian's Wall or the Romans in Bath. A local museum may have some Roman artifacts in their collection.

Possible Visitors
Curator or Education Officer from Museum.
Amateur archaeologist.

Best Time of Year
Any.

ROMANS

Topic ... Turn to Appendix 8

CREATIVE WORK

Listen to written accounts; examine pictures; discuss and then write:

A day in the life of a Roman Soldier.
Everyday life on Hadrian's Wall.

Write poems about cold, dank weather.

Write: A Britain's view of Roman Life and
A Roman's view of British Life.

Talking and Listening

Discuss: Is the Roman Invasion of Britain a fairy story or is it real and factual? How do we know?

Listen to story of Romulus and Remus. Discuss - is this fact or fiction.

Queen Boadicea - fact or fiction?

Talk about how Britain changed during the Roman occupation

INDIVIDUAL ACTIVITIES

Make up individual topic booklets containing stories written and information collected.

Research: Roman Food; town life; Roman villas; dress; Roman army; roads, entertainment; education etc.

Make mosaic patterns from squares of sticky paper or clay tiles painted and varnished.

Make clay models of small Roman pots. Dye sheep wool and experiment with various types of weaving.

Construct models of a Roman road; the inside of a villa; a Roman galley; a chariot; simple battering rams, stone throwing machines and catapults.

END PRODUCT

Display of written and creative work or individual booklets made.

Model of Hadrian's Wall.

Model of Roman Fort or Mile Castle.

Large Time Line which shows when the Romans came to Britain.

Large wall maps showing extent of Roman Empire.

Display of mosaic designs.

Act out a scene depicting the Roman army in action.

PROGRAMME OF STUDY

Pupils should be introduced to the early history of the Briitsh Isles. They should have opportunities to learn how British society was shaped by invading peoples. The focus should be on Roman, Anglo-Saxon and Viking invasions and settlements and on Britasin as part of a wider European world. Pupils should be taught about:

Invasions and settlements from 55 BC to the early eleventh century: The Roman conquest and settlement of Britain; resistance to Roman rule, including Boudicca; Britain as part of the Roman Empire; the departure of the Legions. Anglo-Saxon invasions and settlements, including the rule of Alfred, King of Wessex; the conversion of England by Roman and Celtic Christians.

Viking raids and settlement; Britain as part of a wider Viking world.

Pupils should have opportunitires to study in greater depth one of the three invasions, the motives which prompted it, the way of life of settlers and of the peoples whom they conquered. They should be taught about

Reasons for invasion: The search for land, trade and raw materials.

Way of life of the settlers: Everyday life in town and country; houses and home life; religious life.

The legacy of settlement: Place names and language; myths and legends; styles of art and architecture.

SKILLS TO BE DEVELOPED

Research skills - see Appendix I

Historical Skills

Use words and phrases relating to the passage of time including ancient, medieval, modern, B.C., A.D., Century etc.

Develop a sense of chronology by sequencing periods in history and events within those periods.

Make connections between different periods of historyand different features of past societies.

Be aware of the legacies left behind from a period in history e.g. Florence Nightingale's work improved hospital conditions. Roman constructed roads improved communications.

Investigate differences between versions of past eventsand examine reasons why they differ e.g. World War II memories.

Extract information from and comment on a range of historical sources related to a task e.g. World War II documents, artifacts, pictures, photographs, music etc.

CURRICULUM LINKS

English	-	Write using Anglo-Saxon runes (alphabet)
Science	-	Experiment with different ways of joining wooden sides of cottage models.
Technology	-	Design and make working models of Saxon carts or simple water mills.
Geography	-	Look for Anglo-Saxon place names on a map (e.g. dene = hill, ford = river crossing, ham = settlement, leigh = clearing in the woods, worth = land enclosed by a hedge)
Music	-	
R.E.	-	Investigate Anglo-Saxon pagon Gods and how Christianity finally spread across Britain.
Art	-	Design elaborate Anglo-Saxon brocches and belt buckles.

Invaders &

Settlers ...

(If you have carried out this

WHOLE CLASS ACTIVITIES

Discuss and write briefly about early British History i.e. Stone Age; Bronze Age; Iron Age; Ancient Britons; Romans etc.

Talk about where the Anglo-Saxons came from; why they came and how they lost control of the country.

Discuss the two different types of Christianity which spread across Britain and the Whitby Synod of 664.

Talk about the Sutton Hoo Treasure and speculate who could have been buried.

Make a class model of an Anglo-Saxon farming settlement complete with church, hall, cottages, roads and farmland.

Construct a full size Anglo-Saxon soldier in battle dress.

SMALL GROUP ACTIVITIES

Talk about the way of life of a Monk.

Write simple manuscripts with quill and ink.

Design illuminated letter shapes.

Act the part of archaeologists and examine a bag of artifacts e.g. sword, shoe, cloth, plate, jewelry etc. Speculate who owned these objects and how they lived.

Research and make a calender of seasonal jobs to do on the farm.

Discuss the uses of artifacts in pictures.

Make a map of the seven Saxon Kingdom.

Make a map showing where the Angles and Saxons came from.

STARTING POINTS

Listen to a class novel set in Anglo-Saxon times e.g. 'The Lantern Bearers' by Rosemary Sutcliff.

Visit to a local museum to look for evidence of Anglo-Saxon presence in the area.

Dress in simple cloaks with sword and shield - act out a battle scene.

Build an Anglo-Saxon model village with accurately constructed cottages.

Recommended Reference Books

From Cavemen to Vikings - R. J. Unstead - Pub. by A & C Black.

The Anglo-Saxons Activity Book - British Museum Publications.

The Saxons and the Normans - Paperbird

RESOURCES/EQUIPMENT

Dictionary, Encyclopaedia, slides, posters etc.

A good collection of children's reference books on Roman Times.

A collection of Anglo-Saxon artifacts or reproduction everyday items from Museum Service.

Examples of Anglo-Saxon dress for pupils to dress up.

Archaeology - open-ended computer program about an archaeological dig - Cambridgeshire Software House.

Possible Visits
Local museum to look for Anglo-Saxon remains.
Local church with evidence of Anglo-Saxon remains.
Offa's Dyke.

Possible Visitors
Curator or Education officer from museum.
Amateur archaeologist.

Best Time of Year
Any

ANGLO SAXONS

Topic .... Turn to Appendix 8)

CREATIVE WORK

Listen to written accounts; examine pictures; discuss and then write:

A day in the life of an Anglo-Saxon farmer.
A day in the life of a Monk.

Talking and Listening

Listen to the story of Beowulf.
Listen to stories about King Arthur and the Knights of the round table. Discuss whether fact or fiction.

Listen to stories of King Alfred including King Alfred and the cakes. Discuss whether fact or fiction.

INDIVIDUAL ACTIVITIES

Make up individual topic booklets containing stories written and information collected.

Research: Anglo-Saxon male and female dress; diet; occupations; monks and monasteries.

Design a woollen cloak for export!

Make models of simple ploughs to be pulled by "Britains model horses".

Make a reproduction Anglo-Saxon helmet.

Make reproduction swords and shields,

Make jewelry from clay.

Make model village houses, a church etc for use in whole class model.

END PRODUCT

Display of written and creative work or individual booklets made.

Display of model village typical of the time.

Display of model cottages showing "tongue and groove" type wooden walls and thatched roofs.

Construct a menu of typical Anglo-Saxon food and hold a feast with appropriate entertainment.

Large Time Line showing where Anglo-Saxons are found in British history.

Time Line showng main events of Anglo-Saxon times.

PROGRAMME OF STUDY

Pupils should be introduced to the early history of the Briitsh Isles. They should have opportunities to learn how British society was shaped by invading peoples. The focus should be on Roman, Anglo-Saxon and Viking invasions and settlements and on Britasin as part of a wider European world. Pupils should be taught about:

Invasions and settlements from 55 BC to the early eleventh century: The Roman conquest and settlement of Britain; resistance to Roman rule, including Boudicca; Britain as part of the Roman Empire; the departure of the Legions.
Anglo-Saxon invasions and settlements, including the rule of Alfred, King of Wessex; the conversion of England by Roman and Celtic Christians.
Viking raids and settlement; Britain as part of a wider Viking world.

Pupils should have opportunitires to study in greater depth one of the three invasions, the motives which prompted it, the way of life of settlers and of the peoples whom they conquered. They should be taught about

Reasons for invasion: The search for land, trade and raw materials.
Way of life of the settlers: Everyday life in town and country; houses and home life; religious life.
The legacy of settlement: Place names and language; myths and legends; styles of art and architecture.

SKILLS TO BE DEVELOPED

Research skills - see Appendix I

Historical Skills -

Use words and phrases relating to the passage of time including ancient, medieval, modern, B.C., A.D., Century etc.

Develop a sense of chronology by sequencing periods in history and events within those periods.

Make connections between different periods of history and different features of past societies.

Be aware of the legacies left behind from a period in history e.g. Florence Nightingale's work improved hospital conditions. Roman constructed roads improved communications.

Investigate differences between versions of past events and examine reasons why they differ e.g. World War II memories.

Extract information from and comment on a range of historical sources related to a task e.g. World War II documents, artifacts, pictures, photographs, music etc.

CURRICULUM LINKS

English	-	Write names and messages using The Viking alphabet - the futhark. Investigate how the days were named.
Science	-	Experiment with different materials and mixtures to make wattle and daub walls.
Technology	-	Design and build a model Viking loom. Use it to weave some cloth.
Geography	-	Use maps to discover Viking place names e.g. _____ toft, _____ thwaite, _____ thorpe etc.
R.E.	-	Talk about Viking burial mounds and the sort of things found in them and question why! Discuss Viking Gods.
Art	-	Design and create your own Viking ship figurehead.

Invaders &

Settlers ...

(If you have carried out this

WHOLE CLASS ACTIVITIES

Discuss and write briefly about early British History i.e. Stone Age; Bronze Age; Iron Age; Ancient Britons; Romans, Angles and Saxons etc.

Talk about why the Vikings came; how they conquered; the peace made with King Alfred; the final raid in 1066 etc.

Make a Time Line through history showing when the Vikings invaded Britain.

Make a Time Line showing the main events of the 300 years the Vikings spent in Britain.

Dress a child in Viking costume or armour for others to sketch.

Make a class model of a Viking settlement with groups making various components.

Make a full size mock-up of a Viking warrior complete with armour and weapons.

Devise a menu for and hold a Viking feast.

SMALL GROUP ACTIVITIES

Construct a map of Viking occupied land in Britain.

Draw a plan of a typical Viking settlement.

Construct a map of Viking voyages of trade, raids and settlements.

Make sketches of Viking tools and implements.

Devise a set of instructions with diagrams telling how to build a full size longship.

Examine the finds from a pretend archaeological dig (e.g. costume jewelry, comb, pieces of material, old shoe, coins, cups, bowls, buckets etc). Speculate about what sort of person would have used these items.

Make replica highly decorated Viking weapons and helmets.

Make model buildings to be included in a class model Viking settlement.

Carve out Runes on slabs of clay.

STARTING POINTS

Listen to a class novel set in Viking times e.g. 'Axe Age, Wolf Age' by Kelvin Crosley Holland or 'Viking Dawn' and other stories by Henry Treece.

Visit to local museum to look for evidence of Viking presence in the area.

Act out a Viking raid on a British settlement.

Discuss their reasons for these actions.

Recreate a Viking saga in a school play.

Recommended Reference Books

From Cavemen to Vikings - R.J. Unstead - Published by A & C Black.
The Vikings - Stanier & Sutton - Pub. by BBC Books in association with Heritage Books.
The Vikings Activity Book - D.M. Wilson - British Museum Publications.
The Vikings - S. Barton - Ladybird Books.

RESOURCES/EQUIPMENT

Dictionary, Encyclopaedia, slides, posters etc.
A good collection of children's reference books on Roman Times.
Usborne cut-out models - "Make this Viking Settlement" - possibly assembled by a parent.
Local museum loan of artifacts or replicas.
Viking England - a suite of four computer programs - available from Fernleaf Educational Software Limited.
BBC Zig-Zag - 5 programmes on The Vikings.

Possible Visits
Local Viking remains - the best being the Jorvik Viking Centre in York. A local museum may have some Viking remains in their collection.

Possible Visitors
Curator or Education Officer from museum.
Amateur archaeologist.

Best Time of Year
Any.

VIKINGS

Topic .... Turn to Appendix 8)

CREATIVE WORK

Listen to written accounts; examine pictures; discuss and then write:

A visit to a Viking Market.
The first Viking raid on Lindisfarne from
(i) a Viking point of view (ii) a monk's point of view.
A day in the life of a Viking boy.
A Viking warrior's diary.
A Viking poem or saga.

Talking and Listening
Talk about the "Law" and how disputes between people are settled. Discuss how this was done in Viking times.
Talk about Norse Gods and legends.
Listen to some Viking Sagas. Discuss how we know about these.
Listen to the story of King Alfred and the cakes.
Debate if you think this is true or false.

INDIVIDUAL ACTIVITIES

Make up individual topic booklets containing stories written and information collected.

Research: different Viking occupations and trades; Viking dress for farming and fighting; country and town homes; trade with other countries.

Make models of Viking trading and fighting ships.

Make copies of Viking jewelry.

Make clay models of Viking chessmen and learn to play the game.

Make copies of Viking memorial stones.

Draw a cross-section of a Viking longboat and label the parts.

Attempt to make a simple Viking shoe from cardboard.

END PRODUCT

Display of written and creative work or individual booklets made.

Display a model of a Viking settlement complete with longships in the harbour.

Large Time Line showing when in History the Vikings came to Britain.

Large maps showing Viking voyages of exploration and settlement.

A Viking Saga acted out for school and parents.

Large pictures of men and women depicting typical dress and family life.

PROGRAMME OF STUDY

(This work should be carried out with mapD from the N.C. Geog. guidelines as well as with other appropriate atlases and maps).

Children should be able to locate on a map the constituent countries of the U.K. They should be taught that their own locality can be considered as part of a region and learn of the geographical features of the home region. (The definition of the region should be determined by the teacher - see guidelines).

Children should describe the features and occupations of other U.K. localities studied and compare them with those of the local area. They should investigate why people move homes e.g. change of employment etc., why different means of transport may be used for different purposes and how people and goods transfer from one means of transport to another. They should study how the extraction of natural resources affects environments e.g. quarries, mining etc and the differences between manufactured goods and natural resources.

SKILLS TO BE DEVELOPED

Research Skills - See Appendix 1

Geographical Skills -

Use pictures to identify features/find out about places and then describe using geographical terms.

Interpret symbols, measure direction and distance, follow routes and describe the location of places using maps.

Make representations of real or imaginary places; make and use maps of routes, and sketch maps of small areas showing
the main features and using symbols with keys.

Use the eight points of the compass.

Determine the straight line distance between two points on a map.

Use letter and number co-ordinates and four-figure grid references to locate features on a map.

Locate their position and identify features outside the classroom using a large-scale map.

Identify features on vertical aerial photographs and match them to a map.

Use maps to find out where features are located and where activities take place.

Find information in an atlas using the index and contents pages.

CURRICULUM LINKS

English	-	Attempt a few words of the Welsh language. Talk about its origin.
Maths	-	Use the scale on maps to calculate distances between major towns.
Science	-	Research how T.V communications are sent from region to region.
Technology	-	Design a set of clothes to cope with the extremes of U.K. weather conditions.
History	-	Talk about the history of the Union Jack.
Music	-	Listen to, learn and comment on traditional English/Welsh/Scottish/Northern Irish music.
R.E.	-	Talk about the different types of churches found in your locality.
P.E.	-	Role play the movement of a parcel from one end of the country to the other.
Art	-	Make a class mural depicting U.K. industries and way of life.

THE U.K.

REG

(If you have carried out this

WHOLE CLASS ACTIVITIES

Make maps of the U.K. based on Map D in the Geog. Guidelines. Talk about regions and mark your region on the map.

Discuss the physical features of your region and some of the major industries. Talk about dialect, local customers etc.

Carry out a survey of jobs carried out by parents.

List the products manufactured locally. In groups research how and where other products are made. Compare local products with other areas.

Carry out a survey of reasons for people moving home.

Make a U.K. map and mark on different sources of energy. Discuss how this may effect occupations.

Talk about how coal is mined and what it is used for. Talk about natural resources and man-made products.

SMALL GOUP ACTIVITIES

Make a U.K. map and mark on counties.

Plan a journey for a student, a businessman, a family of four from Glasgow to London, bearing in mind cost and amount of luggage to be carried.

Research the journey of a parcel from your home town to the Queen!

Research car making in Sunderland or Birmingham; the Oil Industry in Aberdeen; Coal Mining in South Yorkshire; Steel making in Sheffield; the Chemical Industry in Teeside; Pottery making in Staffordshire; Farming in Lincolnshire; Fishing from Hull and Grimsby etc.

Take a printed map with gridlines and work out the coordinates of your place of study.

STARTING POINTS

Construction of large wall chart or 3D relief model of the U.K. showing physical features.

Talk about U.K holidays and long journeys the children have been on.

Write to a number of large industries up and and down the country requesting information on their products.

Make a visit to a farm or factory to find out which raw materials are used and where finished products are sent to.

Recommended Reference Books
Britain - Maps and Mapwork - Macmillan Education.
Looking at Britain - Gadsby - A. & C. Black.
We Live in Britain - C. Fairclough - Wayland.
Book of Britain - Williamson & Meredith - Usborne.
Welsh for Beginners - Language Guides - Usborne.

RESOURCES/EQUIPMENT

Dictionary, Encyclopedia, slides, posters etc.
A good collection of simple children's reference books about the United Kingdom.
Postcards and photographs.
Catch - a computer simulation about the fishing industry - Pub. by Scetlander.
Wall maps of the U.K. which show cities and towns, rivers and hills, energy, counties, transport etc.

Possible Visits
A visit to a local factory or farm, bus station, railway station, motorway services station or a parcel sorting office.

Possible Visitors
A visitor from another part of the U.K.
A train driver, lorry driver, airline pilot to talk about their work.

Best Time of Year
Any.

AND ITS

IONS

Topic .... Turn to Appendix 8)

CREATIVE WORK

Listen to written accounts; examine pictures; discuss and then write:

A travel brochure to attract people to visit the region you live in.
A typical day at the factory.
A typical day on the railway.
A typical day of an airline pilot.

Talking and Listening

Debate Mr. Blogg's aged 70 having to leave his farm to make way for a new road.
Read Charlie and the Chocolate Factory by R. Doahl - Puffin - and then visit a real factory.
Talk about where we get and how we use fuel and energy.

INDIVIDUAL ACTIVITIES

Make up individual topic booklets containing stories written and information collected.

Make a model of a typical farm, fishing boat etc.

Make or draw a plan of a railway terminal showing how wagons are loaded/unloaded.

Make a model of an airport which shows how planes are loaded/unloaded.

Paint pictures of national flags.

Design a poster to sell goods from a factory you have visited or know about.

Make a U.K. map and mark on rivers and hills.

END PRODUCT

Display of written and creative work or individual booklets made.

Hold a class game of "Battleships" where individual pupils call out the co-ordinates of their place of study and class members mark on their own maps.

Report back to the class a summary of your information collected about your place of study.

Large 3D relief model of the United Kingdom.

Make a frieze which shows how one set of raw materials are turned into a useful product.

Make a frieze of a busy motorway, railway station or airport.

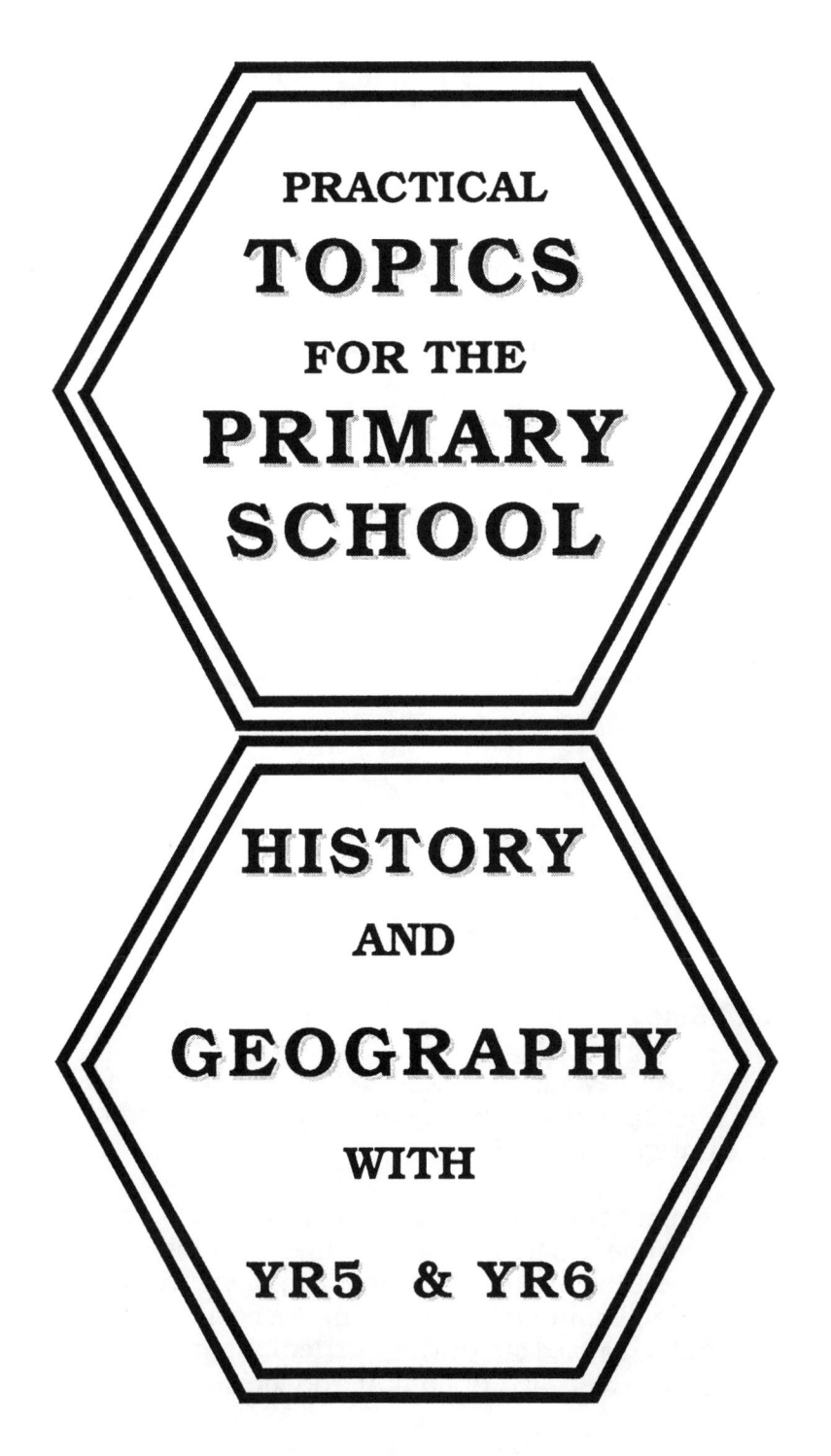

PRACTICAL TOPICS FOR THE PRIMARY SCHOOL

HISTORY AND GEOGRAPHY WITH YR5 & YR6

HISTORY & GEOGRAPHY WITH YEARS 5 & 6 (Upper Juniors)

At this level the topics should have a definite bias towards either History or Geography. The themes will last approximately half a term and should include research and practical activities. Six themes in a <u>two year cycle</u> require three major Humanities topics to be carried out each academic year. Science and Technology topics will be carried out during the remaining half terms.

Humanities Topics - Years 5 & 6 - Two Year Cycle

History	Geography	R.E.
Tudor and Stuart Times	The European Connection	
Victorian Britain	World Navigators - Old & New	

Weighting Within a Topic

The Geography Topic "World Navigators - Old and New" is made up of 50% Geography Study of a locality in an economically developing country and 50% History Core Study Unit 6 - Exploration and Encounters 1450 to 1550.

The details for the development of an additional History topic - Britain since 1930 - have also been included in this book. The author envisages this topic as combining 50% Core Study Unit 4 Britain since 1930 and 50% History Supplementary Study Unit - Section B - a local history study of the community's involvement in a particular event (in this case World War II). This topic should be carried out during curriculum time allocated to language work (speaking and listening) and be based upon oral and local history.

Details for the development of two topics biased towards R.E. will be found in Practical Topics for the Primary School - Part 3 - available later.

Weather studies "How site conditions can influence surface temperature and affect windspeed and direction. Measure and record the weather using direct observation and simple equipment. Recognise seasonal weather patterns; learn about weather conditions in different parts of the world e.g. in polar, temperate, tropical desert and tropical forest regions. Learn that rivers have sources, channels, tributaries and mouths, that they receive water from a wide area, and that most, eventually, flow into a lake or the sea; that rivers, waves, winds and glaciers erode, transport and deposit materials" - from the Georgraphy programme of study - should be included in the Natural Science Topic "Weather Watching".

Earth studies "Investigate and compare the colour, texture and organic content of different types of soil. Study the nature and effects of earthquakes and volcanic eruptions, and how the latter produce craters, cones and lava flows" - from the Geography programme of study - should be included in the Technology Topic "Underground".

Art and Craft

As well as the many creative activities possible within the topics, specific Art and Craft lessons may be used to teach techniques such as fine drawing, use of colour, clay work, tie and dye, marbling, printing, use of different media such as pastels, chalks, charcoal, needlework and textiles etc. An excellent resource for the non-specialist Art teacher which follows a scheme is "Teaching Art in Primary Schools" by Geoff Rowswell published by Collins Educational.

Information Technology (Computer Studies)

Pupils should have the opportunity to use Information Technology for:
(a) Word processing and simple desk top publishing.
(b) Data-base work.
(c) More advanced graphics.
(d) Control technology.
(e) Musical composition.
(f) Adventure programs.

PROGRAMME OF STUDY

Pupils should be introduced to key issues and events in Tudor and Stuart times. The focus should be on the way of life of people at all levels of society and on well-documented events and personalities of the period. Reference should be made to the histories of England, Wales, Scotland and Ireland.
Pupils should be taught about:

Rulers and court life
Tudor and Stuart rulers. Major events, including the break with Rome, the Armada, Gunpowder Plot, Civil War and Restoration.
The Courts of the Tudor and Stuart monarchs.

People in town and county
The way of life of different groups in town and country: trade and transport: the great Plague (1665) and the Great Fire of London (1666)

Scientific and Cultural Achievements
Scientists and their discoveries, including Newton: architects and their buildings: music and drama, including Shakespeare.

Exploration and empire
Explorers and their voyages, including Drake and Raleigh: the beginnings of the British Empire.

Religious Issues
Religious changes: religion in everyday life: King James's Bible.

SKILLS TO BE DEVELOPED

Research skills - see Appendix I

Historical Skills -

Use words and phrases relating to the passage of time including ancient, medieval, modern, B.C., A.D., Century etc.

Develop a sense of chronology by sequencing periods in history and events within those periods.

Make connections between different periods of history and different features of past societies.

Be aware of the legacies left behind from a period in history e.g. Florence Nightingale's work improved hospital conditions. Roman constructed roads improved communications.

Investigate differences between versions of past events and examine reasons why they differ e.g. World War II memories.

Extract information from and comment on a range of historical sources related to a task e.g. World War II documents, artifacts, pictures, photographs, music etc.

CURRICULUM LINKS

English	-	Read some simple extracts from the works of Shakespeare.
Maths	-	Calculate the stores required to feed a ships crew for a fixed period of time.
Science	-	Experiment with getting tall sailing ships to stay upright in water. Investigate the problems of carrying cannon.
Technology	-	Design and make a bed with a rope matress large enough for a doll. Make appropriate bed clothes for it.
Geography	-	Map the voyage made by Drake in the Golden Hind.
Music	-	Attempt to sing Elizabethan madrigals. Listen and respond to Music from Tudor England.
R.E.	-	Examine copies of King James's Bible. Talk about how it came to be written.
Art	-	Make silhouette pictures of the Great Fire of London.

TUDOR &
TI

(If you have carried out this

WHOLE CLASS ACTIVITIES

Make a time line which shows where Tudors and Stuarts fit into British history.

Make a time line which shows the rulers of the period.

Talk about the main events and personalities including Monks, Abbeys, Henry VIII and the destruction of the monasteries.

Discuss how the Stuarts took over from the Tudors.

Discuss the Civil War and the execution of the King; the Commonwealth, Mary and William of Orange; the control of Parliament and the uniting of England and Scotland.

Use model ships made individually to recreate a scene from a battle with the Spanish Amada.

Use model houses made individually to recreate a scene from the Fire of London. Include streets, churches, shops etc.

Make full size pictures of a Cavalier and Roundhead.

SMALL GROUP ACTIVITIES

Map the route of the Armada and mark positions of wrecked ships.

Investigate the story of the Armada from the Spanish and the English point of view.

Design a game in which sailing ships engage in battle around the coast of Britain.

Plan the equipment needed for a group of people to colonize a new country.

Make a ship's log for a voyage of discovery.

Carry out the Mary Rose computer simulation.

Devise a document written with a quill and signed with a seal.

Make a strip cartoon telling of the dissolution of a monastery.

STARTING POINTS

Listen to a class novel set in Tudor or Stuart times. e.g. *A Cold Wind Blowing* - Barbara Willard; *When Beacons Blazed* - Hester Burton; *The Queen Elizabeth Story* - Rosemary Sutcliff; *Escape of the King* - Jane Lane.

Make simple costumes and fight a mock battle between Roundheads and Cavaliers on your school field.

Through drama explore the different tasks involved in sailing and living in a Tudor ship.

Play ring a roses and discuss the connection with the plague.

Recommended Reference Books

Tudors & Stuarts - R. J. Unstead - Published by A & C Black.
The Tudors - T. Wood - Paperbird (Ladybird)
The Stuarts - T. Wood - Paperbird (Ladybird)
The Spanish Armada - Ladybird.

RESOURCES/EQUIPMENT

Dictionary, Encyclopaedia, slides, posters, etc.
A good collection of children's reference books on Tudor and Stuart times.
Postcards of Tudor portraits available from the National Portrait Gallery.
Cassette of Tudor England music - available from Longman Primary Music, Longman House, Harlow.
Mary Rose Computer program.
Local documents from Tudor Times from your County records Office.

Possible Visits
Remains of a monastery. A Tudor building. A local museum/antiques shop to examine Tudor/Stuart artifacts. A local church with Tudor/Stuart architecture.

Possible Visitors
The curator/education officer of a local museum.
A local historian or antiques dealer.

Best Time of Year
Any.

STUART TIMES

Topic ... Turn to Appendix 8

CREATIVE WORK

Listen to written accounts; examine pictures; discuss and then write:

The voyage of the Golden Hind.
The plague hits our family.
The day of the Great Fire in London.
A newspaper report of the Gunpowder Plot.
A day in the life of a monk.

Talking and Listening

Discuss the beliefs of a puritan.
Discuss the basic differences between a Catholic and a Protestant.
Discuss the problems caused to poor people by the enclosure of land.
Discuss why people thought the world was flat.
Debate the rights and wrongs of the Slave trade.

INDIVIDUAL ACTIVITIES

Make up individual topic booklets containing stories written and information collected.

Research: Tudor and Stuart fashion; punishments, pastimes; travel; food; occupations; coffee houses; a famous explorer such as Drake or Raleigh.

Make model Tudor ships similar to those used in the first Royal Navy.

Make model Tudor houses with wooden frames and include a chimney.

Make small clay bricks and with others build an early brick house. Discuss advantages.

Draw a cross-section of a Tudor warship.

Sketch pictures of early fire arms.

Paint portraits of a King or Queen.

Make collage figures for a Tudor scene.

END PRODUCT

Display of written and creative work or individual booklets made.

Large model of Armada sea battle.

Large model of Fire of London.

Frieze of Tudor/Stuart street scene.

Competition to see who has devised the most interesting "Sea Battle Game".

Make a class frieze of the original London Bridge.

Act out a small part of a play by William Shakespeare in Elizabethan dress.

PROGRAMME OF STUDY

This work should be carried out with maps B and D from N.C. Geog. guidelines as well as appropriate atlases and maps.

Children should learn that their own country is part of a continent. They should learn about some of the geographical features of the U.K.; of changes that have occurred as a result of human actions;, e.g. construction of the channel tunnel; study a route linking two places and understand why roads and railways do not always take the shortest distance between the places they link.

Children should study the reasons for different uses of land and for the location of different types of work e.g. sources of power, raw materials, the transport network etc. They should study how the occupations, land-use and settlement patterns of a locality in a European Community country outside the U.K. are related to the area's environment and location.

SKILLS TO BE DEVELOPED

Research Skills - see Appendix 1.

Geographical Skills - see "The U.K. and its Regions."

More able pupils should also be taught to :

Use maps E & F in the N.C. Geography Guidelines.

Use conventional 1:50,000 or 1:25,000 Ordnance Survey map symbols with the aid of a key.

Follow a route on an Ordnance Survey map and describe what would be seen.

Use six-figure grid references to locate features on a map.

Interpret relief maps.

Extract information from distribution patterns shown on maps.

Use a map to identify features they have seen.

Use latitude and longitude to locate places on atlas maps.

Recognise that a globe can be represented as a flat surface.

CURRICULUM LINKS

English	-	Make an "English Sayings" dictionary for a continental visitor e.g. Raining cats and dogs means ....
Maths	-	Research European currencies and calculate how much of each you could exchange for £1.
Science	-	Build a balloon powered balsawood hovercraft that works.
Technology:	-	Design and sketch an alternative to the channel tunnel.
History	-	Research the history of the E.E.C.
Music	-	Listen/learn/comment on some traditional music.
R.E.	-	Sketch and name some European places of worship.
P.E.	-	Movement based on channel tunnel excavations.
Art	-	Attempt to recreate the paintings of past European masters.

THE EU CONNE

(If you have carried out this

WHOLE CLASS ACTIVITIES

Make individual maps of U.K. marking on the details found on N.C. Geography Guidelines Map D.

Make individual political maps of Eurpe (Map B) marking on seas and country names. Discuss the problems of travelling from U.K. to mainland Europe.

Examine photographs of Dover harbour and the ships/hovercraft used to transport vehicles. Plot their routes on a large scale map. Compare with route taken by "Sally Line". Why is this?

Research the construction of the channel tunnel. What dictated the route? How are the people in Dover affected now and in the future? What is happening to the material excavated?

Look at Dover (or local) large scale O.S. maps to see if railways travel in a straight line. Why not? Describe the route taken. Use grid references to locate some features.

SMALL GROUP ACTIVITIES

Plan a holiday to a European Country. Choose a destination, plan what to take, how to get there and how much it will cost.

Design a travel brochure for a European holiday. Include details about travel, where to stay, itinerary, route and high/low season costs.

Use maps to plot a journey across Europe e.g. Orient Express. Name the countries passed through, describe the scenery and the time taken.

Use slides/postcards/photographs to compare scenes in one country with your own area.

Researh local uses of land and industry and compare with land use and industry in a European region (e.g. Netherlands).

Use latitude and longitude to locate European places in an atlas.

STARTING POINTS

Make a collection and talk about holiday souvenirs, travel brochures, European football teams, newspaper cuttings, national dolls etc.

Construct a giant map of Europe with groups contributing individual countries drawn to same scale and fitted together like a jig-saw.

Make a large 3D model of Europe showing seas, main mountain regions and national boundaries.

Listen to "The Wheel on the School by Meindert de Jong..

Recommended Reference Books
Europe - Maps and Mapwork - Macmillan Education.
The World - Maps and Mapwork - Macmillan Education.
Usborne Guides to France, Spain etc.
Usborne Picture Word Books - French, German etc.

RESOURCES/EQUIPMENT

Dictionary, encyclopedia, slides, posters, videos etc.
A good collection of children's reference books concerning Europe in general and one country in particular (e.g. The Netherlands).
A collection of postcards and photographs.
Atlases and globes.
Continental Newspapers.
Micro Map 1 & 2 - Computer Program which practices map reading skills - Longman.

Possible Visits
A local supermarket to chat which foods come from European countries.
A local travel agent to find out how to get to Europe - a local bank to learn about European currency.

Possible Visitors
A European national to speak about their country or to talk to the children in their native language.
A parent with holiday slides of a European visit.
A construction worker from the channel tunnel.

Best Time of Year.
Any.

ROPEAN CTION

Topic .... Turn to Appendix 8)

CREATIVE WORK

Talk about, look at pictures, act out and finally write:

A holiday diary for a European holiday.
An adventure on the Orient Express.
A short conversation written in French.
Poems about a train journey.
A "James Bond" type adventure involving a chase across Europe using various means of transport.

Talking and Listening
Talk about and role play some of the problems you would encounter shopping in a country where you could not speak the language.
Listen to some simple language tapes and learn a few "French" words. Try communicating with a friend. Talk about Rotterdam as a place of "trade". What do we mean by this?

INDIVIDUAL ACTIVITIES

Make up individual topic booklets containing stories written and information collected.

Research everyday way of life, jobs, foods eaten, housing, spare time activity, homes etc in one European country.

Research how climate varies across Europe and discuss how this effects the way of life.

Make drawings/paintings of famous landmarks, national flags, national dress etc.

Copy designs of European food wrappings.

Paint designs on plates from continental pottery.

Answer quiz questions using an atlas.

Learn to play the French game of boules.

Make a map of European air routes.

END PRODUCT

Display of written and creative work or individual booklets made.

Large class map of one European country containing rivers, mountains, cities etc.

A continental meal or food tasting session.

Make a large scale mock up of the channel tunnel with a model railway.

Hold a competition to see who can build a model ferry which will hold more cars than any other.

Make a collage of a busy port.

Make a frieze of a typical rural dutch scene.

Make a working model of a roll-on-roll-off ferry terminal.

PROGRAMME OF STUDY

Pupils should be introduced to life in Victorian Britain and its legacy to the present day. The focus should be on men, women and children at different levels of society in different areas of Victorian England, Wales, Scotland and Ireland, and on how they were affected by industrialisation.
Pupils should be taught about:

Economic Developments
Steam-power, industry and mass production: child labour. New forms of transport, including railways, the growth of towns, trade and the growth of the British Empire.

Public Welfare
Public health, education.

Religion
The importance of religion to Victorians.

Scientific and cultural achievements
Inventions and scientific discoveries: buildings and public works: art, photography and literature.

Domestic Life
Victorian families: houses and home life: leisure and pastimes.

SKILLS TO BE DEVELOPED

Research skills - see Appendix I

Historical Skills -

Use words and phrases relating to the passage of time including ancient, medieval, modern, B.C., A.D., Century etc.

Develop a sense of chronology by sequencing periods in history and events within those periods.

Make connections between different periods of history and different features of past societies.

Be aware of the legacys left behind from a period in history e.g. Florence Nightingale's work improved hospital conditions. Roman constructed roads improved communications.

Investigate differences between versions of past events and examine reasons why they differ e.g. World War II memories.

Extract information from and comment on a range of historical sources related to a task e.g. World War II documents, artifacts, pictures, photographs, music etc.

CURRICULUM LINKS

English	-	"Copper Plate" handwriting lesson.
Maths	-	Calculate what could be bought for 1d. Examine the wages earned in different sectors of society.
Science	-	Investigate how a Steam Engine works and the uses made of the invention.
Technology	-	Use the computer to enter and use Census data in a data base program. Design and build a water powered mill wheel.
Geography	-	Examine maps of the British Empire, and of railway expansion in Great Britain.
R.E.	-	Sunday Schools as the beginning of day schools. The Temperance movement, Lord Shaftsbury's reforms.
P.E.	-	Drill.
Music	-	Recreate a Music Hall scene.
Art	-	Make drawings and paintings of scenes from Victorian Times. Sew samplers of religious texts.

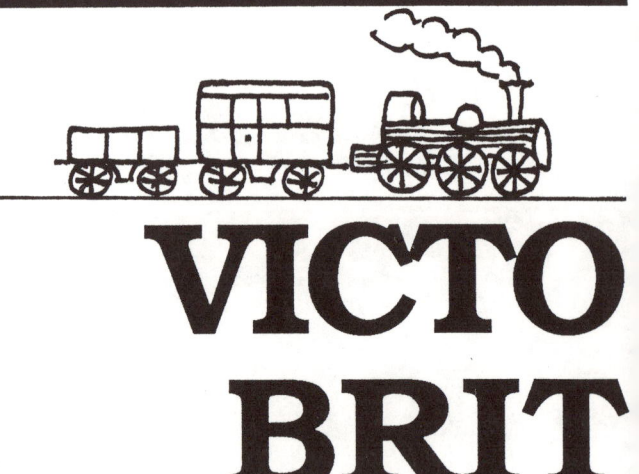

VICTO
BRIT

(If you have carried out this

WHOLE CLASS ACTIVITIES

Discuss and note on long-term time line where "Victorian Times" fit into historical order.

Visit a Victorian display/museum collection. Discuss and illustrate carefully a number of typical artifacts.

Visit an area which contains "Victorian" and contemporary architecture - compare and note the differences.

Carry out a close procedure exercise to give written overview of the period.

Run a model steam engine in the classroom and discuss what it needs to work. Talk about uses in railways, farming, ships and factories. Talk about expansion of industry in towns.

Dress in Victorian dress for a day/morning. Act out a classroom scene. Write on slates, chant tables etc. Write with pen and ink in well using joined up style.

Do simple sums with pounds, shillings and pence etc. Play appropriate playground games.

SMALL GROUP ACTIVITIES

Compare photographs of a street scene 100 years apart - discuss and note the differences.

Research the dates of various inventions of the period, illustrate and arrange in chronological order.

Examine and discuss selected events from an old school log book.

Examine old documents e.g. maps, plans, census returns etc which give clues to how people lived.

Study and answer questions from old photographs, posters and reproduction newspapers.

Examine and talk about unusual Victorian artifacts - speculate about their use.

Construct a model Music Hall/Theatre - use cut out figures on wire to act out a play.

Construct a model showing the inside of a Victorian mansion and another showing the inside of a terraced house.

- 90 -

STARTING POINTS

Make a collection of Victorian artifacts.

Listening to a novel based in Victorian Times e.g. 'Tom's Midnight Garden' written by Phillipa Pearce.

Discuss some of the main events and changes in Victorian Times.

Examine new inventions of the era and discuss how they changed peoples lives.

Borrowing Victorian style costumes from a museum and act out roles or model for class art work.

Recommended Reference Books

Queen Anne to Queen Victoria - R. J. Unstead - published by A. & C. Black (still an excellent resource!)

How We Used to Live 1850 - 1901 - F. Kelsall - published by Simon & Schuster

Two Victorian Families - S. Wagstaff - published by A & C Black

RESOURCES/EQUIPMENT

A good collection of school reference books on "Vicotorian Times". Slides, posters, Computer Data Base program (e.g. Grass, Our Facts, Factfile etc). Census data taken from 1841, 51, 61, 71, 81 and 91. Old photographs and etchings.
Reproduction Victorian O.S. maps and street plans.
Reproduction Newspapers and post cards.
I.T.V. How We Used to Live Video - The Victorians 1874 - 87.

Possible Visits
Wigan Pier Museum, a Victorian Cottage, Victorian Mansion or any "Victorian Theme" museum. An area of town/city where Victorian architecture predominates or an antique shop.

Possible Visitors
The curator of a local musuem.
A local historian or antiques dealer.

Best Time of Year
Any.

RIAN AIN

Topic ... Turn to Appendix 8

CREATIVE WORK

Talk about, look at pictures, act out and finally write.

A day in the life of a working child.
A day in the life of a Victorian classroom.
A day in the life of a soldier nursed by Florence Nightingale.

Drama:
Act out a day in a Victorian School either in your own classroom or in a local museum.

Talking and Listening
Listen to a novel based in the era. Discuss the ways of life depicted.
Compare a day in the life of a Victorian maid with a day in the life of a wealthy young lady.
Discuss the types of public health connected with various living conditions. Compare with today.
Discuss the work of Florence Nightingale and the changes that followed.
Discuss some of the major events of the period, inventions, wars and the expansion of trade.
Discuss the great changes created by increased mobility due to the invention of railways.

INDIVIDUAL ACTIVITIES

Make up individual booklets containing accounts of visits made and research carried out.

Research using appropriate reference books graded for reading ability: Penny Post; the Great Exhibition at Crystal Palace; Railways; Bicycles; Steam - Ships; Street Life; Leisure and pastimes.

Construct a quantity of terraced houses (from a simple plan) plus other models for a Victorian street scene.

Cut out clothes to dress a card outline Victorian Doll - research appropriate colours and materials to make the dresses as accurate as possible.

Sketch in great detail some Victorian artifacts.

Sketch and paint items to be included in a class street scene.

Make a peg doll.

END PRODUCT

A Victorian fashion parade.

A model Victorian Street scene with rows of terraced cottages, a factory building, shops, one or two Victorian Mansions and appropriate street transport.

A collection of Victorian toys or artifacts displayed as if in a museum.

Display of written and creative work or individual booklets made.

Large "Time Chart" depicting main events of the period or a chart which shows where "Victorian Times" fit into British history.

Full size Victorian shop front for role play in the classroom.

HISTORY PROGRAMME OF STUDY

Pupils should be introduced to the developments which brought Europeans into contact with American peoples. The focus should be on the reasons for the voyages of exploration, the Spanish voyages, the nature of Aztec civilisation, the encounter between the two cultures and its results.
Pupils should be taught about:

Voyages of exploration
Descriptions and maps of the world in the late fifteenth century; the search for a route to the Spice Islands, including Columbus's voyages; navigation on trans-oceanic voyages and life on board ships on trans-oceanic voyages.

Aztec Civilisation
Montezuma and the Aztec Empire; the Aztec way of life; Aztec gods and religious practices; Aztec crafts and technology; Aztec art and architecture.

The Spanish conquest
Differences between European and Aztec civilisation; motives for the expedition of Cortes; the Spanish conquest of the Aztec Empire; the legacy of the Spanish conquest of the Aztec Empire; the creation of the Spanish American Empire; the growth of trade between the Old and the New World.

HISTORY SKILLS - see Victorian Britain.

GEOGRAPHY PROGRAMME OF STUDY

This work should be carried out with map C from N. C. Geog. guidelines as well as appropriate atlases, maps and globes.

Children should examine the impact of landscape, climate and wealth on the lives of people in a locality of an economically developing country e.g. Brazil. They should investigate recent and proposed changes as a result of human actions, evaluate the impact of changes on a settlement and understand that conflicts can arise over the use of land. They should consider why some parts of the world contain very few people while other parts are densely populated. They should learn about the importance of fresh water sources and means of ensuring a reliable supply.

Children should study ways in which people look after and imporve the environment and consider why some types of environment need special protection. They should learn some of the ways in which damaged environments can be restored.

GEOGRAPHY SKILLS - see The European Connection.

CURRICULUM LINKS

English	-	Write a letter to a newspaper giving reasons for saving the Amazon Rain forest..
Maths	-	Invent a board game about a sea voyage using co-ordinates.
Science	-	Make a bottle garden to recreate a "rainforest type" environment.
Technology	-	Design and build an effective blow pipe or a hammock for a doll.
Music	-	Listen and respond to examples of South American music.
R.E.	-	Debate the moral issues behind exploration, particularly the slave trade.
P.E.	-	Movement work based on a fierce storm at sea.
Art	-	Make an Amazon Rain Forest collage.

WORLD NA
OLD an

(If you have carried out this

WHOLE CLASS ACTIVITIES

Explore a local park and make maps of it.. Include symbols and a scale. Compare results.

Use atlases to practice using latitude and longitude.

Use nets to construct a globe from a flat sheet of card. Colour as a world map.

Discuss in detail the conditions Columbus lived in during his voyages.

Study the way of life of the Aztec people before western influences.

Talk about Cortes' battle with the Aztecs.

Investigate the modern country of Brazil and the way of life of people in the city and in the country including coffee production.

SMALL GROUP ACTIVITIES

Research and devise an equipment list for a voyage of exploratin in a 15th Century ship.

Draw a world map and plot the four voyages of exploraation made by Columbus.

Make maps of the West Indies and mark how close Columbus came to the Amazon.

Make a political map of South America.

Make a physical map of South America.

Plan a modern equipment list for an exploration of the Amazon Rainforest.

Draw a diagram showing different jungle layers.

STARTING POINTS

Study world maps, globes and atlases. Talk about Equator, Tropic of Cancer and Capricorn.

Learn about latitude and longitude and simple navigation.

Ask "Who drew the first map?"

Look at early world maps and discuss the "Flat Earth Theory".

Investigate Christopher Columbus' voyages of exploration.

Talk about who makes the same journeys now and why?

Investigate Brazil and the Amazon Rain Forest.

Recommended Reference Books

Christopher Columbus - Marshall Cavendish Discovery Collection.
Great Civilisations - The Aztecs - Ladybird Books.
Living in Aztec Times - R J Unstead - A. & C. Black.
Let's go to Brazil - K. Lye - Franklin Watts.
Amazon Adventure - B. Huntley - Collins.
Young Geographer Investigates - Tropical Forests - T. Jennings - Oxford Books.

RESOURCES/EQUIPMENT

Directory, Encyclopaedia, slides, posters etc.
A good collection of children's reference books concerning Christopher Columbus, the Aztecs, South America, Brazil and the Amazon Rainforest.
Replica world maps from the 1500's.
A set of atlases and globes; political and physical.
Large scale maps of the West Indies/Mexico area.

Coffee - a computer simulation - Pub. by Storm.

Possible Visits
A local park, school grounds or other open space to be explored and mapped.

Possible Visitors
Someone who has explored distant places!

Best Time of Year
Any.

CREATIVE WORK

Talk about, look at pictures, act out and finally write:

Surviving a sea voyage to the new world.
The story of an Indian "discovered" by Columbus.
Write the story of Percy Fawcett (an Amazon explorer who never returned)
A South American Indian's view of Western Civilisation!

Talking and Listening

Talk about why Christopher Columbus made his voyages of exploration. Compare with why people travel to South America now.
Talk about how the landscape, climate and wealth of our country influences our way of life.
Compare this with the influences on the way of life of an Amazon Rainforest tribe.
Talk about siting a village and the importance of a fresh water supply.

Topic .... Turn to Appendix 8)

INDIVIDUAL ACTIVITIES

Make up individual topic booklets containing stories written and information collected.

Research: Life on board a 15th Century ship, the Aztec way of life, the Spanish invasion, life in Brazil today, the nature of the rainforest and the environmental problems connected with it.

Make a model of a Caravel (Portugese ship).

Design a terrible sea-monster of unknown waters.

Research how Indian tribes still live in the forest and how modern life is affecting them.

Make a model Concorde, Jumbo Jet and/or airport.

END PRODUCT

Display of written and creative work or individual booklets made.

Class frieze depicting events that happened to Christopher Columbus.

A class model showing sailing ships landing in the fifteenth century and modern planes landing at an airport in the twentieth century.

Design a "Save the Rainforest poster" for a competition.

Make a large class world map with various voyages of exploration marked on.

Make a display depicting the Aztec way of life.

PROGRAMME OF STUDY

Pupils should be shown how to trace connections between the present and events in Britain's recent past. The focus should be on major events and developments and on the way of life of different social groups in England, Wales, Scotland and Ireland since 1930.

Economic Developments
The decline of heavy industries; the growth of new industries, changes in transport.

The Second World War
The impact of the Second World War (1939 to 1945) on Britain.

Social Changes
Changes in the role of men and women and in family life; immigration and emigration.

Scientific Developments
Inventions and discoveries; concerns about the environment.

Religion
Religious changes and their effect on everyday life.

Cultural Changes
Popular culture, including fashion, music and sport; the impact of radio, the cinema and television; changes in architecture.

SKILLS TO BE DEVELOPED

Research skills - see Appendix I

Historical Skills -

Use words and phrases relating to the passage of time including ancient, medieval, modern, B.C., A.D., Century etc.

Develop a sense of chronology by sequencing periods in history and events within those periods.

Make connections between different periods of history and different features of past societies.

Be aware of the legacies left behind from a period in history e.g. Florence Nightingale's work improved hospital conditions. Roman constructed roads improved communications.

Investigate differences between versions of past events and examine reasons why they differ e.g. World War II memories.

Extract information from and comment on a range of historical sources related to a task e.g. World War II documents, artifacts, pictures, photographs, music etc.

CURRICULUM LINKS

English	-	Write articles for a class newspaper based on one day during the period.
Maths	-	Carry out simple calculations using pounds, shillings and pence. Compare imperial and metric weights.
Science	-	Compose a typical war time menu and test classroom reaction to contents.
Technology	-	Design and construct a model prefabricated house which can easily be assembled on a new site.
Geography	-	Make a map of the countries invaded by Germany during the Second World War.
Music	-	Hold a "Juke Box Jury" type quiz show and evaluate examples of popular music from different decades.
R.E.	-	Discuss feelings of bereavement felt by a family on receipt of a "killed in action" telegram.
Art	-	Recreate war time public information posters.

BRITAI

19

(If you have carried out this

WHOLE CLASS ACTIVITIES

Make a Time Line which shows major events and inventions over the last sixty years.

Talk about oral history and different interpretations of similar events.

Devise appropriate questions to ask someone who was a teenager/young person during the 30's; 40's; 50's; 60's; 70's; 80's; etc. Test your questions on friends. Consider arrangements e.g. meeting place; how to make a person relax;; being sensitive etc. Carry out a number of interviews (at least two different people for each period in time).

Talk about and collect other examples of local history covering the period.

Make a presentation to the school/hold an exhibition for parents using information collected from local sources.

SMALL GROUP ACTIVITIES

Listen to oral history tapes from one period. Examine for different points of view. Speculate how these may occur. Research which is probably most accurate.

Listen to two different accounts of one specific event. Construct a newspaper report from the information.

Edit one or two interviews using two tape-recorders. Add your own commentary to make an interesting item for a local radio station.

Edit a tape. Collect war time pictures and artifacts etc. Use tape and collection to make an interesting corner in an exhibition.

Examine war time photographs. Use tape recorders to create a short story complete with sound effects for a radio station.

STARTING POINTS

Listen to a class novel set around the time of the Second World War e.g. 'The Silver Sword' by Ian Serraillier pub. by Puffin Books or 'Carries's War' by Nina Bawden - Pub. by Puffin.

Watch the I.T.V series 'How We Used to Live'.

Dramatise a mock battle based on Second World War facts or a mock evacuation to the country.

Examine wartime School Log Book/Registers.

Make a collection of World War II artifacts and photographs. Set up a museum in the classroom.

Recommended Reference Books

The Twentieth Century - R. S. Unstead - Pub. by A. & C. Black.
Into Modern Times 1901 - 1945 - T. Wood - Pub. by Paperbird (Ladybird)
How We Used to Live 1936 - 53 by F. Kelsall - Pub. by Simon and Schuster.

RESOURCES/EQUIPMENT

Dictionary, Encyclopaedia, slides, posters etc.
A good collection of children's reference books on recent British and world history.
A tape-recorder and microphone.
How We Used to Live - 1936 - 53 - a Yorkshire Television Series.
Reproduction newspapers depicting important events.
Collection of popular music from different decades.
A collection of World War II postcards/cuttings/artifacts.
Archive wartime sound recordings.

Possible Visits
Old people's home to interview some of the residents.
A local antique shop. A local museum to examine artifacts.
Local reference library or newspaper office.

Possible Visitors
A parent/friend who was a teenager in the 1930's; 1940's; 1950's; 1960's; 1970's; 1980's.
A parent/friend prepared to talk about World War experiences. Someone who has emigrated to another country. Someone who has immigrated to our country.

Best Time of Year
Any

N SINCE

30

Topic ... Turn to Appendix 8

CREATIVE WORK

Listen to written and oral accounts; examine pictures; discuss and then write:

A description of devastated buildings and families after a bombing raid.

A letter home after being evacuated to the country.

Attempt simple war time poems.

Talking and Listening

Talk about evacuation of children during World War II - how would you feel about it?
Talk about spending nights sleeping in a cold damp air-raid shelter during the blitz.
Talk about black out, rationing, taped glass windows, lack of road signs and other everyday differences.
Discuss changes in attitudes following the Second World War.
Discuss how people spent evenings without television.

INDIVIDUAL ACTIVITIES

Make up individual contributions to a school presentation or a classroom exhibition.

Research orally people's experiences of changes in transport, dress, diet, cinema, radio and television etc..

Make individual collage pictures to be included in a Time-Line of fashion.

Make models/pictures of planes, ships and cars showing changes through the decades.

Make model houses to be used in class street scene.

Paint replica coronation souvenirs.

Make sketches showing the changes in a person from 1930 to 1991.

END PRODUCT

Display of written and creative work or individual booklets made.

A mock up of the inside of a wartime shelter or period scene from a typical home.

A display of children's toys - now and then.

Large Time Line across the classroom wall displaying events and items connected with each decade.

Make a model of a street scene after a bombing raid.

Hold a presentation for the rest of the school using examples of local evidence collected.

Hold a local history exhibition for parents.

SELECTED BIBLIOGRAPHY

Early Years

Tina Bruce (1987) Early Childhood Education - Hodder and Stoughton.
D Fontana (1984) The Education of Young Children - Blackwell.
The Early Admission to School of Four Year Old Children (1987) Lancashire County Council.
G Barrett (1986) Starting School: An Evaluation of the Experience A.M.M.A
P P Lillard (1972) Montessori - A Modern Approach - Schocken Books - New York.
K Manning & A Sharpe (1977) Structuring Play in the Early Years at School - Ward Lock.
Mollie Jenkins (1973) School Without Tears - Collins.

Topic/Project/Thematic Work in General

Jan Stewart (1986) The Making of the Primary School - Croom Helm, London.
P Rance (1968) Teaching by Topics - Ward Lock Educational.
D Wray (1987) Teaching Information Skills through Project Work.
Bradley/Eggleston/Kerry/Cooper (1985) Developing Pupils Thinking Through Topic Work: A Starter Course - Longman for S.C.D.C.
R Lane (1981) Project Work in the Primary School - Preston C.D.C.
P Bell (1985) History, Geography, Science, Nature and R.E. Primary School Topics - A Skills Approach - Preston C.D.C.
J Makoff L Duncan (1986) Display for all seasons. A thematic approach to Infant Teaching - Belair Publications Ltd.
H Pluckrose (1987) What is Happening in our Primary Schools.

Subject Disciplines
J Blyth (1988) History 5 - 9 -Hodder and Stoughton.
Geography from 5 to 16. Curriculum Matters 7. (1986) H.M.S.O.
Lancashire Looks at.... Science in the Early Years (1986) Lancashire County Council.
Discovering an Approach. Religious Education in Primary Schools, (1977) Macmillan Education for Schools Council.
G Read, J Rudge, R B Howarth (1987) The Westhill Project R.E. 5 - 16 Mary Glasgow Publications Ltd.
Design and Primary Education (1987) The Design Council.

National Curriculum
English in the National Curriculum - D.E.S. -Pub H.M.S.O.
Mathematics in the National Curriculum - D.E.S. - Pub H.M.S.O.
Science in the National Curriculum - D.E.S. - Pub H.M.S.O.
Technology in the National Curriculum - D.E.S. - Pub H.M.S.O.
History in the National Curriculum - D.E.S. - Pub H.M.S.O.
Geography in the National Curriculum - D.E.S. - Pub H.M.S.O.
Aspects of Primary Education:
The Teaching and Learning of Science - H.M.I.
The Teaching and Learning of History and Geography - H.M.I.
The Education of Children Under Five - H.M.I.

PRACTICAL TOPICS FOR THE PRIMARY SCHOOL

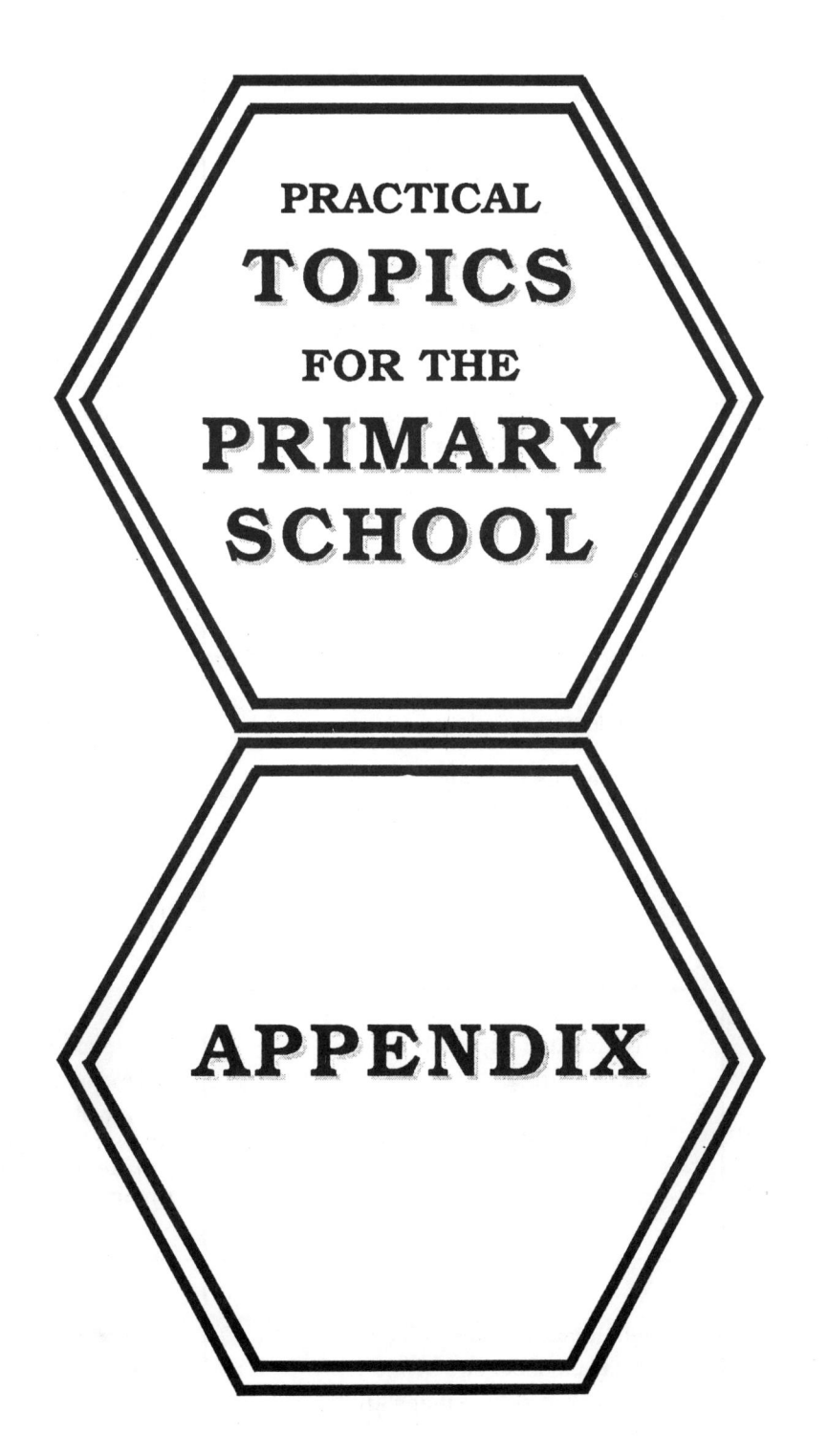

APPENDIX

Appendix 1

RESEARCH SKILLS To be developed in all topics	Nursery/Reception	Years 1 & 2
	The child should be able to:	The child should be able to:
OBSERVATION	- make observsations first hand from a variety of objects, displays, pictures, walks etc. with some guidance as to what to look for.	- collect information by looking at pictures, simple reference books, objects, displays etc.
REFERENCING	- recognise that print is used to carry meaning. - talk about the content of an illustrated non-fiction book. - ask questions.	- read and understand straight forward signs, labels and notices. - demonstrate knowledge of the alphabet in using word books and simple dictionaries. - find the right page in a book. - ask questions of older people.
SPEAKING & LISTENING	- participate in group activities - participate in imaginative play - listen and respond to stories and poems. - follow instructions	- participate as speakers and listeners in a group. - describe an event - listen attentively to stories and poems. - listen, talk and ask questions with the teacher. - follow instructions.
WRITING/ RECORDING	- use pictures, symbols or isolated letters, words or phrases. - to communicate meaning. - draw pictures - make simple models.	- write simple sentences independently. - draw pictures - draw plans and diagrams. - make picture graphs. - make simple models.
INTERPRETING INFORMATION	- talk about pictures, objects, displays, books, etc. - talk about simple maps and picture charts.	- describe the main features in a picture or objects. - interpret picture maps, picture graphs and simple plans.
PREDICTING & HYPOTHESISING	- talk about "what may happen next" during story time.	- make simple predictions following observations. eg. what could happen next?

Appendix 1 (Continued)

Years 3 & 4	Years 5 & 6
The child should be able to:	The child should be able to:
- collect information from a wide variety of sources: objects, pictures books, filmstrips, slides etc.	- select appropriate information from a wide variety of sources: objects, pictures, books, maps, filmstrips, slides etc.
- collect information from books and other sources. - choose a suitable book from a number of books. - use a contents page.	- select relevant information from books and other source. - use an index. - use the reference section in a library. - use an encyclopaedia.
- give an account of observations and experiences. - speak in front of others. - contribute to a joint discussion. - question. - listen. - follow instructions.	- be fluent in describing and recounting. - give an account in a logical sequence. - make relevant comments. - discuss and present a reasoned argument. - question and draw conclusions. - listen. - follow instructions.
- write an account of observations and experiences - make visual representations. - make block graphs, charts and diagrams - make models. - present neat, well set out work.	- write an account of logical sequence. - present a reasoned argument. - present neat, well organised written work. - choose the most appropriate method of recording and illustrating work. - work with other children to produce a group study. - use tables, charts, diagrams, graphs, drawings and models to supplement written work.
- interpret maps, plans, diagrams, tables, charts etc. - analyse information at a simple level (answering simple questions; what does it mean? Why?). synthesise information (use several sources to obtain information e.g. a picture and a map.	- interpret information from several sources. - recognise that there is more than one point of view. - notice inconsistinces. - make judgement about authors, dates of publication assessing fact and opinion, accuracy of source, relevance of information gathered. - make generalisations; offer alternative explanations. - synthesise information; producing coherence from several sources. - draw conclusions.
- make predictions - make guesses about causes.	- make predictions. - attempt to explain causes and effects. - plan the next stage in own research.

Appendix 2 - Sample letter to parents

ANYTOWN PRIMARY SCHOOL

Local Education Authority

Headteacher: Mrs A N Other B Ed.

Tel: Anytown 123456

Roman Road,
Anytown,
Nr Bigtown,
Local.
LEA 123

Date

Dear Parent/Guardian,

     As part of Year 5's work on "Electricity and Magnetism" a visit has been arranged to "Bigtown Power Station". The visit will take place during normal school time on Friday 13th and a packed lunch will be required.

     The subsidised cost of the visit will be £1.00 per child. Under the terms of the Education Reform Act 1988 there is no obligation to contribute to the cost and no child will be omitted from the activity because his/her parents are unwilling or unable to pay.

     However it will be necessary to have substantial parental contributions in order that the activity takes place. If there are insufficient voluntary contributions the event will be cancelled.

     Please let us know if there is a genuine case of hardship. The matter will be dealt with in strictest confidence.

     I look forward to receiving your reply slip as soon as possible.

Yours sincerely,

A N Other
Headteacher

Bigtown Power Station Visit

I am willing to make a voluntary contribution towards the above visit and enclose £1.00 on behalf of _____ (child's name)

signed _____

Appendix 3 - Sample of a Topic Planning Sheet

	TOPIC PLANNER
TITLE	
AIM	What exactly are you trying to achieve by doing the Topic?
RESOURCES	What resources will you need for your activities? ASK FOR ANYTHING! He/She can only say no!
EDUCATIONAL VISIT	Are there any visits you would like to make as part of this topic?

ACTIVITIES   Write down the activities you expect the children to perform.
(It is understood that as the work progresses, new opportunities will be realised and unsuccessful or impractical ones will be discarded).

Appendix 4 - Sample of a Topic Assessment Sheet

ASSESSMENT SHEET			
TOPIC TITLE	Examples from Programme of Study (Content)		Skills to be developed
NAME OF CHILD			
	Level of functioning on a scale of 1 - 5		✓ = has retained x = has not retained ? = not easy to judge

QUESTIONNAIRE
(to be filled in at the end of the Topic)

Which activities went particularly well?

Which activities would you not include if you were to do this topic again?

Was your educational visit worthwhile? (Provided you did one!)

Do you think you achieved your aims?

Appendix 5 - Definitions of National Curriculum Terminology

Aggregation - combining a learner's assessed marks or grades, obtained over a variety of tasks, to give a single mark or grade for reporting purposes.

Assessment - The Secretaries of State may specify, by a Parliamentary order assessment arrangements as they consider appropriate for each national curriculum subject. The Government have decided that assessment arrangements should combine national tests and assessment by teachers.

Attainment Targets - broad descriptions of what children of different abilities and maturities should know, understand and be able to do at particular ages.

Key Stage - a period within compulsory schooling towards the end of which children,s performance against the attainment targets and levels of achievement is assessed and reported. There are four key stages: 5 - 7, 7 - 11, 11 - 14 and 14 - 16.

Level of Attainment - different levels of achievement, reflecting differences in ability and in progress according to age, defined within each attainment target.

Moderation - the process of checking the comparability of different assessors' judgements so as to ensure a common standard.

NCC - National Curriculum Council.

Profile Component - a grouping of attainment targets for reporting purposes (eg. spelling, writing, handwriting). Every attainment target will be assessed, but children's results will not be reported to parents for every atttainment target individually, only for groups of attainment targets.

Programme of Study - what children need to be taught in order to reach the attainment targets at key stages.

Reporting Age - age at which children's performance against the attainment targets and levels of achievement is reported: the four reporting ages are 7, 11, 14 and 16.

SEAC - School Examination and Assessment Council.

Standard Assessment Task - an externally prescribed and externally marked national test which will be applied to test children's achievements against particular attainment targets at different levels.

Statements of Attainment - a specific description of what children should know, understand and be able to do at each level of achievement within attainment targets.

Ten Point Scale - the Government have accepted that children's progress against the attainment targets should be recorded on a
single continuous scale with 10 levels. On this scale levels two, four, five/six and six/seven are to represent the attainments expected of the average child at each of the four reporting ages.

TGAT - Task Group on Assessment and Testing.

Weighting - since results are to be reported against <u>groups</u> of attainment targets (the profile components), it will be necessary for attainment targets to be weighted for purposes of aggregation. Similarly, the <u>profile components</u> identified for any particu;ar subject need to be weighted for the purpose of combining them to produce a single overall mark or grade for that subject.

Appendix 6 - Example of a Library Loan Record Sheet

COUNTY LIBRARY PROJECT LOAN

CLASS: _____

TOPIC: _____

DATE RECEIVED: _____

NO. OF BOOKS: _____

TITLE	AUTHOR	No. of copies	Checked out
		Total returned:	

Appendix 7 - Example of a set of lines used underneath the plain paper

Appendix 8 - What to do with successful Topic ideas?

Teachers <u>should not</u> be continually trying to re-invent the wheel - but <u>should</u> instead be willing to share new ideas and common experiences which others can adapt for use in their own individual circumstances.

Topical resources invite **YOU** to write with your tried and tested pupil worksheet which could possibly be included in a photocopyable resource file. Examples should fit into one of the following 6 catagories:

(1) Whole class activities.

(2) Small group activities (4 - 6 children).

(3) Individual activities.

(4) Extension activities (for more able pupils).

(5) Simpler activities (for less able pupils).

(6) Art/Craft/Creative ideas linked to one of our themes.

For more details write to:

"TOPICAL RESOURCES"
P.O. Box 329
Fulwood,
PRESTON PR2 4SF

Appendix 9

PLAN OF THE TOPICS SUGGESTED IN
PRACTICAL TOPICS FOR THE PRIMARY SCHOOL PARTS 1 & 2

Autumn	People who help us	Birds	Colour	Winter	Homes	The Cafe	Spring				
Ourselves Now!	Around & About Our School		Dinosaurs		My First Six Years		Moving Toys		A Journey to		
Animals & Plants	When Gran & Grandad Were Young		Food		Holidays Abroad		Shadow Puppets		Life in a Castle - Many Years Ago		
Colour & Light	Ancient Civilisations - Egypt & Greece		Build a Better Bridge		Village, Town or City? - a local study		Good Health				
The U.K. & its Regions	Water & Growth		Invaders & Settlers		Energy: Moving Things				In & Around a Wood/Park Wasteland		
Electricity & Magnetism	Tudor & Stuart Times		Underground		The European Connection		Weather Watching				
Victorian Britain & Britain Since 1930 (a language topic)	Road Safety & the Bicycle				Earth in Space		World Navigators - Old & New		In & Around a Pond/Canal/Stream/Sea-Shore		